"This is a beau [...] *what it means* [...] *a book about lov* [...] *every reader will see in her story the truth that family matters."*
—Bret Lott, Author of *Jewel*

"Angie shares her life with honesty and vulnerability and it shines through every page. Abundantly More *is an exquisite book that tells their story in such a powerful, truthful, raw, and tender way! Yes, there is pain and suffering! Yes, He calls us to hard things, but His glory shines so brightly through it all."*
—Adéye Salem, adoptive mother and orphan advocate

"Angie Rylands' story is one of great hope and inspiration even in the face of great grief. Through this book, you will laugh; you will cry; but greatest of all, you will be led to see Jesus and His love and grace through the lives of the entire Rylands family. Thank you, Angie Rylands for honestly and transparently sharing your story of adoption, loss, and redemption with us all."
—Rick Morton, VP of engagement at Lifeline Children's Services and Author of *Know More Orphans*

"Abundantly More *shares more than Angie Rylands' surprising journey. I found the book captivating and was unable to put it down wanting to see what miracle God was going to do in the Rylands family next. It is truly a love story demonstrating how much our God loves us Abundantly More than we can even imagine. A true story of ordinary people that will encourage any reader to trust our good Father more."*
—AnneMarie Ezzo, Co-author of *Growing Kids God's Way, Parenting from the Tree of Life*

Abundantly More

One Woman's Surprising Journey into Marriage, Parenthood, and Widowhood

ANGIE RYLANDS

Palmetto Publishing Group, LLC
Charleston, SC

ISBN-13: 978-1-944313-13-5
ISBN-10: 1-944313-13-3

Table of Contents

Acknowledgements

❧

To Eileen Lass for providing such dedicated and professional editing on this project. Thank you for teaching me to be a better storyteller.

To Dave Wood, my brother in Christ, for your encouragement on this project and for the way you loved Tom. God used you to confirm the writing of this book and to get me started.

To Kim and Annie for the countless hours of conversation as you educated us on special needs adoption. Your advocacy for waiting children in China was what God used to bring four incredible sons into our family.

To Jessica, the Ethel to my Lucy, I love you dear sister. Thank you for being there for me as Tom danced into heaven. Thank you for loving him so. You were so special to Big Daddy. Thank you for the hours you spent pouring over this book and offering humor and advice on this project.

To Sensei Lin Beets and David Hearne, and your amazing wives, for standing alongside our family through triumph and tragedy. For being godly models of Christ's love in many tangible ways for our sons. Thank you for living out the promises you made to Tom and for demonstrating how the body of Christ is to serve others. I know Tom was proud to call you both brothers as am I.

To my precious boys, Colin, Connor, Cameron, Cooper and Tommy, you are the most precious of God's gifts to me. Each one of you was intentionally placed by God into our family and He has used you to teach me many lessons. I love each of you with my whole heart and can't wait to see what *Abundantly More* God has in store for you.

Introduction

When I think back over the years since marrying Tom Rylands, it is almost surreal to me the path that God chose for our family. It was a path that was such a grand departure from any plans that we had for ourselves. When Tom, 28 years my senior, and I approached marriage, neither of us had plans to parent. Tom had been privileged to raise two daughters in his first marriage, and as he was in his fifties when we fell in love, he had no desire to "start over" with more children. He loved being Dad to his married daughters, but felt it was time to slow down and enjoy a new phase of his life. For myself, then in my late twenties, and being crazy in love, raising children wasn't a pressing need, so I readily agreed that we could be a happy family without children. That, in a nutshell, was *our plan*. It was a tidy plan. And as a self-proclaimed Type-A, "tie-a–bow-on-it" sort of gal, I liked tidy.

God's plan, as is often the case, wasn't tidy. God had planned for us to parent, and not just one child, but five! I never imagined in my wildest dreams that I, the oldest of five siblings myself, would ever be the mother of five! To me, that was just crazy. Even as a child, I often questioned whether my parents were a little nuts for having so many kids themselves, especially in light of the challenging financial years we endured together. Tom would say that this is a perfect example of God's infinite sense of humor! And if there was ever anyone who understood humor, it was Tom Rylands! Rest assured, the irony is not lost on me! Looking back, I can remember many times when I thought, "Lord, You must be joking!"

Now in my forties, I look back at that twenty-something girl and laugh about all I thought I knew so clearly. Then again, that is the beauty of maturing and allowing God to grow us. None of us sees the future that God has in store, and despite our best intentions, we rarely get it "right" apart from His guidance and our willingness to submit to His will. Ephesians 3: 20-21 says, "Now to him who is able to do far more abundantly than all that we ask or think, according to the power at work within us, to him be glory in the church and in Christ Jesus throughout all generations, forever and ever. Amen." What I didn't know was that a few short years later, shortly after our marriage in 2001, everything would change. That was the beginning of the sharp left turn God had orchestrated for me and the life that He had planned; a life full of joy, laughter, surprises, financial hardships, great love and deep sorrow, a life that would lead me to complete dependence on Him. This was, for our family, the "abundantly more" that the scriptures spoke of. My prayer is that our story will speak to, convict, encourage or bless you in a way that comes directly to you from God.

CHAPTER 1

Not Your Typical Love Story

I vividly remember the school assembly. The students at Grant Elementary filed into the cafeteria and sat Indian-style on the cold floor, excited to hear from the Band Director of Wilson Junior High School. Today was the day we would learn about all the instruments we could learn to play when we were promoted to seventh grade. I had always loved music and while extracurricular activities were usually out of reach for me due to the added expense, we did have a cornet that belonged to my father as a child. It was beautiful and it was my ticket into the band. From the age of ten, I began taking lessons once a week in that same cafeteria. The following year, I entered the junior high band. About halfway through the year, my band director pulled me aside and asked if I'd consider switching to the French horn. I agreed to discuss it with my Dad and did so right after school. There are some things in childhood that fade away from your memory, despite every effort to retrieve them, but not this conversation. I still remember my Dad asking me one simple question. "Angie, do you think you will ever want to go to college?" At ten years old, I wasn't quite sure what this had to do with my instrument question, but I answered yes. He replied, "Then you need to switch to the French horn. Good trumpet players are a dime a dozen, but a good French horn player can go to college for free." So, that settled it. As soon as I learned that the school would loan me a horn, I switched mid-year to learn the French horn and never looked back. And, yes, it did pay for college. Score one for Dad!

Playing in the band and singing are among my earliest and strongest childhood memories. I knew I would study music in college. Then I'd become a band director. And that is precisely what I did. In fact, for much of my life, I've mapped out a plan and followed it, as close to the letter as humanly possible.

Right out of college, I began teaching. My first job, a total train wreck, lasted a year. It was in a tiny Virginia town that I can't bring myself to name. That's how bad it was to work there. I was under constant attack from boosters and stereotypical "soccer moms" who wanted their child to be in the spotlight all the time. As a new teacher, I sought support from my administration that never came. Picture an old, run-down high school in a rural area where the newspaper still covered family reunions and every single speeding ticket! In the midst of a very challenging year, in a town that felt like a fish bowl, where every move I made was known and discussed throughout the town, there was one family who loved me well, the kind of friends who poured Christ's love into my life. They invited me to worship at their church and they had a home-cooked meal ready whenever I needed it. Now many years later, and separated by several states, these friends are still very dear to my heart.

During these years as a music teacher I met and eventually married the love of my life, Tom Rylands. Like me, Tom was a musician, having played in bands his entire life. There was an instant magnetism about him. He was funny and approachable. As I grew to know him, I saw his unique ability to attract people and make them feel important. Pardon the analogy, but Tom was the kind of guy who could have told you to go to Hell and you would have run home to pack! People just wanted to please him. He was so kind and encouraging that you just wanted him to be proud of you. You had a deep desire to prove that his faith in you wasn't in vain. He could rally people to his way of thinking in a way that wasn't forced. He didn't need to pull rank often because folks just wanted to be on his team.

Despite our age difference, Tom and I loved one another fiercely. There was not one day of our marriage that I doubted his commitment or love for me. In fact, I know Tom would have laid down his life for me. He was a rare breed of man ("A dying breed," he often said). He was an old-school gentleman who taught me how a lady should be treated. I remember walking down a narrow sidewalk with him once when he hopped down into the street and began walking on my right side. When I asked him why, he said, "A lady never walks unprotected from traffic." For some, perhaps this would have been an insignificant gesture, but for me, it was one of many times when Tom showed with his actions that I was precious to him.

In January of 2001, Tom and I married in Richmond, Virginia. An unusual couple, an unusual wedding. It was a Thursday, the five-year anniversary of the day we met. Dates have always been meaningful to us, and we didn't want to pass up this anniversary of meeting one another, so we married almost immediately after becoming engaged. In fact, my wedding dress hadn't even arrived yet, but once we realized that this anniversary was approaching, we decided that we didn't care about our attire and we moved ahead with our ceremony with only a few family members and friends. I wore a wine-colored dress

I'd purchased for another event and carried a modest bouquet of flowers and my mother's small, pink Bible. My sister Amy wore a coordinating dress and stood by my side as my maid of honor. Without all the typical fanfare, the ceremony was short and sweet and remains the most perfect, most under-planned day of my life.

About ten months after our wedding, Tom and I traveled to Rhode Island to attend his 40th High School reunion. Yep, Tom Rylands attended his 40th High School Reunion with his just-turned-30-year-old bride. It was the most beautiful time of year in Rhode Island. The colors were magnificent! Even in Virginia we rarely saw the colors we witnessed in New England that year. The reds were deeper, the yellows more vibrant and the oranges richer than anything I'd ever seen. Everywhere we went, I was captivated by the majesty of God's creation. The strong breeze off the Newport coast was exhilarating during the warm afternoons. Though it was very early in our marriage, for Tom this remained the most cherished of our trips together. He was so proud to show me his home and the beauty that surrounded it.

I loved having Tom show me the places that were so dear to him. We visited the high school where he competed as a swimmer and boxer. This school, built in the early 1920s, is still in use today and the only high school in Pawtucket, Rhode Island. In the basement was a full-size pool surrounded by bleachers. The strong smell of chlorine greeted us as we walked inside. It was here that Tom competed for the state swimming championships. We also walked through his college campus in Kingston, RI and ate at his favorite old restaurants. We followed the cliff walk along Narragansett Bay, went to Point Judith Lighthouse, and shared stories of Tom's childhood. I was struck by Tom's love for the water and for New England.

As for the reunion, I was somewhat nervous to walk into a room full of Tom's high school classmates. We always got lots of attention wherever we went, but here I would stand out even more than normal.

We found our assigned seats and Tom began to work the room as only he could. He was so proud to introduce me to old friends and everyone was very polite and kind, despite the shocked looks on their faces! As we sat down to eat, folks relaxed and the jokes began to fly. This was Tom Rylands in all his glory. My husband was the center of every party and had a story for every occasion. He was equally comfortable in a tuxedo or overalls, and social settings never rattled him. He could be formal and appropriate when needed and completely hysterical and irreverent a moment later. He was more than a joke teller; Tom was a joke weaver. He started every joke as if it were a true story. "Did I tell you about the time I…?" Or, "Did you hear about the young man who…?" These "stories" were Tom Rylands' trademark. So, in his classic style, sitting at the reunion table, he began, "You know, we had a lot to think about before we decided to get married, what with the big age difference and all. I went to the doctor to discuss my health before proposing and he informed me that at my age, sex could be fatal. 'Well,' I replied to the doctor, 'if she dies, she dies!'" Tom's classmates roared with laughter, I blushed and shook my head in disbelief, and the elephant in the room was gone!

Our life together was nothing Tom or I could have scripted. None of the plans we'd made came to pass. If they had, I shudder to think how things would have turned out. When you allow God to take over the writing and directing of your personal life story, and lean into the promises of His Word, the final result can be quite remarkable. God truly worked a miracle in our lives, blessing us abundantly more than we could have dreamed, and boy, am I grateful!

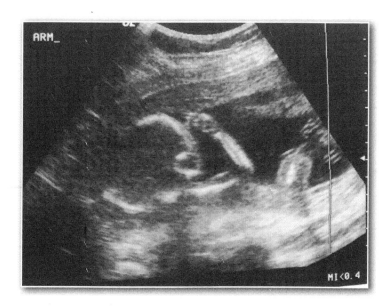

CHAPTER TWO

The Baby Bug

*O*vernight, our tidy plans felt terribly wrong. Like a storm that comes without warning, I became that hysterical woman who cried through every diaper commercial. It became so bad that I had no choice but to tell my dear husband that I wanted a child. But a child was not part of our plans. We'd discussed it long before we married. We had agreed. It was a daunting conversation but one that God used to grow my patience and dependence on Him.

It took time to muster the courage to tell Tom about my growing desire to be a mother. I was not at all pre-pared for his answer. When I finally shared my feelings, Tom's knee-jerk reaction shattered my heart into a thousand pieces. "Honey," he said, "if you are serious, then I'm afraid you are going to have to get a different husband." I was devastated and angry that God would place such a strong desire in my heart and then not have the decency to get my husband on board!

Here I was, barely married a year, and my husband was already talking about our relationship not working out. I was lost as I tried to reconcile my desire for a child with my husband's lack of any such desire. I mentioned that I'm a "get my own way" girl. I remember as clearly as if it were yesterday, how tempting it was to prey on his deep love for me whenever the opportunity presented itself. I knew that eventually, with enough persistence, I could get him to cave. I knew that I could get my way if I worked hard enough on manipulating his feelings. He loved me that much, and I knew it. Thankfully, this would not be the first or the last time that God would intervene and protect me from myself.

Late one evening, Tom, who normally stayed up much later than I to read, went up to bed, but I was oddly restless and not ready to lie down. Sitting in front of the fireplace I heard from the Lord. He showed me the train wreck that lay ahead if I pushed my desires ahead of His will. He showed me a clear picture of families that do not have two equally committed parents on board to tackle the challenges of raising a child. It was like watching a tragic movie in my head and I knew that if I did anything outside of God's perfect timing, this would be the future of my family. I immediately got on my knees at the round maple coffee table where Tom himself had learned to walk, and asked the Lord to protect me from my own selfish desires. I knew all too well what I was capable of and I did not want to grow our family that way. I chose instead to trust that God had placed this mother's heart in me and that when it was time, His time, that He would fulfill this plan in my life.

The months that lay ahead were hard, but the Lord continued to encourage me and He continued to grow Tom and me together in our marriage. But, this was not the time for a quick answer to prayer. No, the Father in His perfect plan called me to wait. He called me to trust Him. But, He didn't leave me completely alone in the wait.

One Sunday morning, from the orchestra pit where Tom and I both sat, the Holy Spirit whispered in my ear. Here was another of those rare times in my life where I knew I was hearing from the Lord. He said so clearly to my spirit, "If you will wait on me, I will give you the desires of your heart." I had no idea that he had abundantly more in mind for me than just that one answered prayer. At the conclusion of the service, I was happier than I had been in months. I was filled with joy that the Lord had not forgotten me. This was not just some generic promise that I was reading in the Bible that may or may not have been meant for me. This was a direct message from a loving and intimate God for Angie. I walked out of church that day smiling from ear to ear. It was a gorgeous spring morning. As we made our way to the car, I remember thinking that God had painted that crystal blue sky just for me. I had no more idea when I would become a mother than I had three hours before, but I knew that it would come to pass and much like Mary, I pondered these things in my heart.

On Sunday, March 16, 2003, during a time of corporate prayer, Tom stepped out of the orchestra pit and knelt at the altar to pray. I remember it because it was not at all common. The orchestra normally played softly during this prayer time and so we would not typically stop for prayer, but today was different. Back at home, Tom asked me to join him on the sofa. He took my hand and with a very serious expression, he said, "I am still scared to death about this, but I believe that the Lord wants us to have a child." Despite the Lord's promise to me, hearing those words was almost too wonderful to believe. This man, who a year before thought perhaps we'd made a mistake in marrying, was now saying that he was ready to step into fatherhood. Then I understood why I had to wait. The Lord needed to work in Tom's heart before he could answer my prayer.

Once Tom shared his decision with me, that was all I needed. I immediately set out planning our little family. I went shopping! I didn't wait for any pesky details like getting pregnant. As far as I was concerned, this was a done deal and I was willing to take that to the bank, or in my case, to Babies R Us! It was all I could do to not start painting a nursery.

I'd love to tell you that nine months later we held that little bundle of joy in our arms, but it wasn't that easy. By the time Tom and I were in agreement, I was thirty-one years old. Though I still felt young, I quickly learned that thirty-one is, for many women, past their peak fertility. I never imagined that I would not get pregnant right away. After all the prayer and waiting, I truly thought that God would respond with a baby immediately. Once again, we were to wait. All these many years later, I realize that waiting on anyone, even the most trustworthy Lord of the universe, is not my best event.

We began that all too familiar fertility dance. Maybe you know it: the two weeks on, two weeks off dance. The waiting to ovulate, then waiting for confirmation dance, or rather the monthly disappointment that followed time and again. It is an emotional journey that causes so many couples to question the Lord, and to even despise their own bodies for not complying with their wishes. I was no exception. Month after month we waited. We consulted doctors and of course, we prayed. After months of purchasing ovulation kits and pregnancy tests, one day.... oh I still remember that day! It was February 12, 2004. I took yet another pregnancy test and much to my amazement, it was positive! I stood there, alone in our bathroom, staring at the two most beautiful little lines!

I twirled around the room! I then fell to my knees once again, thanking God for His faithfulness and answered prayer. It finally happened. I was pregnant!

My mind raced to come up with the perfect way to tell Tom. After all, if ever there was a time for some pomp and circumstance, this was it! I decided to take him to our favorite little Greek restaurant in Richmond. It had the best food in town and had been a special place for us. I wanted this to be a surprise, so when Tom came home from work that afternoon, I told him I was taking him out for an early birthday dinner. I made him dress up and off we went.

The quaint restaurant felt intimate as Frank Sinatra crooned through the room. The lighting was dim and the atmosphere quiet. Shortly after we were served our drinks, I slipped away to find our waitress. You see, I wanted her to deliver his "present" to the table on her tray. Though her English wasn't the best, I was able to explain that inside the black velvet bracelet box I'd handed her was a positive pregnancy test! When she realized what I was up to, she squealed so loudly I thought for sure Tom would hear. A moment later, I returned to the table and tried to resume a normal conversation.

The next few minutes dragged as the butterflies in my tummy were swirling. Then, I saw her heading for our table with my black velvet box. As she placed the tray in front of him, he looked confused. I explained that his birthday present was inside and that he should open it. I imagine he was thrown for a moment getting a nice jewelry case, as this would not have been a typical birthday gift. I held my breath as I watched him open the case. Having no idea what I was up to, and given that the lighting was quite dark, it took him a few seconds to wrap his head around what exactly he was looking at.

I had a moment of panic. What if I'd been fooling myself and I had actually forced this on him after all? What if he wasn't happy? What if he freaked out? Had I only heard what I wanted to hear? Then, there it was. That smile. That shocked, excited, almost doubtful smile that covered his face and instantly allayed my fear and confirmed his true heart for this much-anticipated life inside me.

Suddenly, he placed the case back on the table, grabbed my hand, and asked me to dance. In the middle of the restaurant, we danced to some Sinatra and the entire restaurant exploded in applause as he announced that he was going to be a Daddy again.

I forget what we ate that night, but I remember some details. I remember our decision to keep this news to ourselves for awhile, just in case. I remember that just after leaving the restaurant, Tom grabbed his cell phone and called my mother and blabbed our good news! I remember that this was but the first of many phone calls he made that night to friends and family who would support us and celebrate with us. I remember laughing at his suggestion that we "keep this to ourselves" when he couldn't go ten minutes without gushing our good news. That's what I remember.

Over the course of my pregnancy, the Lord continued to lead us in a new and exciting direction. After several successful years working at Capital One Financial, I realized that I didn't want to miss one second of this child's life, so despite our agreement that I would continue working once our child came, I again approached Tom with a new plan. You do recall how things worked out the last time I surprised him with a change of plans? Well, this time was a little better. After the initial heart failure wore off, he realized that if God had brought us here, after all we'd been through, He would surely make a way for us financially if He wanted me to be a full-time stay-at-home mom.

It was the first time that I would leave a great career position for my family, but it would not be the last. Tom had accumulated twenty-five years in public service to the state of Virginia as a school administrator, and was eligible for a full retirement. He realized that if he retired and began receiving these benefits, he could still work full-time in another state. This would require a move, but would give us the possibility of both a full-time school administrator's salary as well as retirement income which was sufficient to meet our financial needs once I left my job. After a long search, Tom was offered the position as Principal of a Title I school in Charleston, South Carolina. It was not unlike the schools in which he'd served for so many years in Virginia.

Within days of the job offer, Tom reported to work in Charleston. That left me, seven months pregnant, to stay behind to sell our house and car. I also managed the packing, loading and shipping of all our worldly possessions with a small army of helpers from our church. In the meantime, Tom found a room to rent and dove into a new school year. For six weeks, he slept on an air mattress and waited for my arrival.

I will never forget the emotions that overtook me as I watched our home being packed up. Our precious church family showed up in force with lots of muscle to load our PODS on a nasty, rainy day. When everything was packed, and our friends had gone home, I was alone in that big brick home. The only belongings left were an air mattress, folding lawn chair, a 13" television, a telephone and a suitcase of maternity clothes. Due to some obligations, I was not scheduled to leave for South Carolina for another two weeks.

For the previous three years, I had performed with a women's vocal ensemble called *Treasures of Grace*, and the six of us had become very close. We were scheduled to record our second album that month. The first was a collection of praise and worship hymns and this new one would be a Christmas album. Can you picture me at this cover photo shoot, seven months pregnant, wearing a red velvet maternity dress…in August? Well, in case you can't, let me just say, it was hot! I'm pretty sure even our non-pregnant members were warm in their winter outfits!

Next it was time to record the album. The studio was about an hour's drive from town and we all left bright and early. After recording for over eight hours, we were completely spent. I grabbed fast food on the way home so I could go straight to bed. I called Tom to say an early good night and to share about our day in the studio. Completely fatigued, the emotional roller coaster of pregnancy got the best of me and I just lost it. I was alone, pregnant, exhausted, sleeping on an air mattress, and did I mention I was pregnant? Tom calmed me down and encouraged me as best he could from two states away. I had wanted to be strong for him and not let on that I was struggling. I knew he had so much on his plate, looking for a home for us and juggling a new job in a struggling school.

I had barely gotten off the phone when I heard the doorbell ring. It was just starting to get dark and I looked awful from all the crying. I walked downstairs to answer the door and was greeted by one of Tom's good friends who lived a few streets away. In his hands were two DQ Blizzards! He said, "A little birdie told me that you could use some cheering up." I felt badly that I didn't even have a chair to offer him, so we sat down on the staircase, eating our blizzards and talking. Needless to say, it did cheer me up! This is the kind of love and thoughtfulness that would characterize my years with Tom.

Once the album was complete, and my work obligations were met, I was reunited with Tom and we prepared to welcome our son.

On October 29, 2004, in beautiful Charleston, SC, our little miracle baby came along, our precious Tommy. Tom was 61 years young and I was, for most first-time moms that I knew, older at 33. Boy, was I in love with that baby! Having nothing with which I could compare this experience, I can't say this is unusual, but what I will say is that I knew, or at least I thought I knew, that this would likely be the only child I'd ever have, so I was not going to miss or mess up one single moment of motherhood!

CHAPTER THREE

Our Tommy

❧

*Y*es, I was that mother. I was going to be perfect. Then life happened. That life involved a new home in a new city in a new state with a new baby!

This was not so welcome to the accomplished, corporate, high energy, problem solver that I had always considered myself to be. Tom went back to work and there I was, home alone with the world's most colicky child! Tommy cried constantly and nothing that I read, tried or even imagined would soothe him for long. Even the old "ride in the car" trick failed because he hated that car seat! Taking him anywhere was pure torture -- for both of us! There were days that I questioned my sanity and my ability to do what seemed perfectly natural to every other woman on the planet. How was it possible that this incredible miracle could be such a colossal pain? We were in full-on survival mode! Every outing started with screaming and ended with me blasting the radio to drown out his screams. At times I feared I'd run off the road. The most blessed event was when he cried himself to sleep from pure exhaustion.

Now, before you bury my inbox with hate mail, know that I desperately loved this child. I tried everything I knew to comfort him, but at the end of the day, if there was someplace we had to be, this was the only way to get us there. Until.....

It happened. One blessed day, the "heavens open up and you hear the angels singing" kind of day, with a little creative engineering on my part, I successfully introduced little Tommy Rylands to his thumb! That's right. His perfect little thumb. And don't tell me about his future orthodontic issues. I would have paid for braces ten times over! He was only a few weeks old, but once I saw the magic of that little thumb, I would have propped his arm up myself to keep him quiet and content. Soon he was able to get his own thumb into that pretty little mouth. It was a glorious new day for our family of three.

This was just one of the challenges the Lord brought our way that would teach me the depths of my own inadequacies. Parenting has a way of highlighting our weaknesses, doesn't it? Well, we survived those early months of infancy and lived to tell the tale. You might know the exhaustion that comes with a fussy baby, but can you imagine doing it at sixty-one years old? Tom

Rylands was a champion in my book: a fully committed, diaper-changing, bath-giving, lullaby-singing champion. Tommy's bedtime quickly became Tom's thing. In part, he took this over to protect my sanity. But also bedtime had become a special time of bonding for my two men. Tom, among his many other talents, was a poet, and he wrote a bedtime song for Tommy called *The Sandman*. For years, he would sing this to Tommy as he rocked him in the glider or in later years, as he sat beside him in his toddler bed.

Sandman

When the sandman puts sand in your eyes,
All your dreams will be filled with surprise,
Full of wonder and puppies and joy
For my sweet little blue-eyed baby boy.

When my sweet baby lies in his bed,
He has Elmo snuggled up by his head.
With horsey asleep by his side,
In his dreams they can romp, play and ride.

When the sun comes to wake up the day,
Tommy's strong and he's ready to play.
He greets the morn and the hours God gives,
And Dad will love him as long as he lives.

Despite the doctor's assurance that Tommy's colic would last about three months, our little guy was a born overachiever. But, one day, at about five and a half months old, it all stopped. It just stopped. No more crying, no more gassy tummy. There, right before our eyes, was the happiest, most perfect little baby boy!

It didn't take long for little Tommy's personality and giftings to become apparent. He was charming, bright and articulate. When he was eighteen months old, we started to realize that he was, as my Dad would have put it, somewhat smarter than the "average bear." He was speaking to us in grammatically correct sentences. Did we realize that we had an adventure ahead? Honestly, we just chalked it up to both of his parents being well edu-cated and having an above-average grasp of the Queen's English. After all, isn't that what's supposed to happen when you read to your young child? But, we would soon learn that it was more than that. We would soon learn what a truly gifted child looked like and we'd also soon learn that with special gifts (read: special needs) come special challenges and opportunities.

In the next few years, Tommy's love of language and exploration grew and we began, at the age of two, to teach him basic phonics. He loved learning so much that every exchange became a game to him. We would ride around in our minivan playing the "spelling game" together. Once he had mastered his letter names and sounds, it was fun for him to spell simple three-letter words as I pronounced them from the front seat. One afternoon, I heard a little voice from the backseat as we sat at a stop sign. "S.T.O.P. Stop!" Yes, my little two-year-old blondie was reading the street signs! By his third birthday, he was reading small books from the Hooked on Phonics curriculum and loving it! We were the family that had to punish our toddler by taking away his "learning games!" As I write this I'm struck by the fact that this is still our most effective disciplining tool for Tommy, now eleven years old. The boy loves to read. Constantly.

I'll never forget him waking us up on a precious Saturday morning before seven wanting to "play learning games" with us. Now, remember it was a *SATURDAY* morning. I was not basking in the glow of a brilliant child who wanted to learn. No, I was tired and whiny because my kid wouldn't SLEEP in on the weekends like I wanted him to. The "adorable factor" had long since worn away and while I did still love to watch his little mind expand, I wanted him to kindly reserve those urges for a rainy Sunday afternoon when it didn't interrupt our slumber.

As Tommy grew and we grew to understand the way his mind worked, we identified what seemed like gaps. But, since he was so far above in almost every cognitive area, it was honestly hard to tell what was a real gap. In certain arenas, he was a "typical" toddler. In others, it was like conversing with a teenager in a tiny body. In still others, we wondered if perhaps he had actual deficits. So, after lengthy discussions, we decided to have our almost-five-year-old son formally tested. We didn't care what the results were, as long as they helped us to understand our son and meet his individual needs. What an eye-opener! We learned that while Tommy was functioning at a very high rate in nine out of ten of the cognitive function areas, there was one, executive processing speed, where he was just barely above his chronological age. At first, I was relieved to learn that there were no deficits. What we later grasped was that for a kid like Tommy, whose other cognitive processes were functioning anywhere from two to ten years beyond his actual age, to have an executive processing score right at age level was, in essence, the same as having a learning disability. He became frustrated when his brain worked faster than his mouth. He could not articulate answers as fast as he could come up with them. We were told that unless we were able to help bridge that gap, Tommy would always struggle. Kind of crazy, isn't it? This kid who was reading by his third birthday and accurately diagramming sentences at age five, had a mild learning disability under all those layers of smarts!

Suffice it to say, not many of our friends felt much sympathy for our plight of meeting the needs of this crazy smart little boy. After all, being extra smart isn't a handicap! Or is it?

The journey of the next several years convinced me that so-called "gifted kids" benefit from the same kind of intentional advocacy as those on the opposite end of the learning spectrum. I have often said that a gifted child ought to have his own IEP (Individualized Education Program) just like those with different exceptionalities. So far, to my knowledge, my philosophy has not taken root! The myths surrounding these kids (that they are "easy" or "self-sufficient" or "always get good grades" or "never struggle in school") don't ring true.

In these years, my entire world revolved around that boy! He was remarkable in every way. He was, down to his beautiful blue eyes and blond hair, the precise child I'd prayed for for so long. Yes, I was one who prayed for a boy. A blond-headed, blue-eyed baby boy to be precise. I know that wasn't socially acceptable, but for whatever reason, this was the vision of my child the Lord had brought to my heart and I knew that was the child He had planned for us. Little did I know back then that the Lord was using Tommy to prepare me to parent many other boys, boys with unique and special needs of their own.

CHAPTER FOUR

Life Is Good

When Tommy was about three and a half, Tom accepted a teaching position at a small private school in the country. They couldn't pay much, especially for someone with Tom's years of experience, so they allowed Tommy to attend their K-4 program for free to sweeten the deal.

We were blessed with a wonderful veteran Kindergarten teacher who recognized Tommy's gifts, and was an encouraging and calming influence on his mother! It was stressful having a child with such high academic skills, but who was struggling to potty train! None of his development was typical, so in some respects, he was ahead of the class, but in others, he was behind his peers. There were only eight kids in his class, so he got plenty of attention and personalized instruction while learning the ins and outs of navigating social relationships and structured settings.

It was a challenge for the teacher, however, because Tommy was the only one in the class who could read, so as she was attempting to introduce the class to the alphabet and the basics of phonics, poor Tommy was constantly being shushed as he blurted out answers or read the board aloud for fun.

Tom stayed there only one year before having a major accident and needing to leave his position. It was the summer of 2008 and a dear friend was helping Tom move a piano from our garage into our living room. I was thrilled with the deal I'd gotten on this used piano and I couldn't wait to start teaching Tommy to play. I received a frantic phone call at work telling me that Tom was in the Emergency Room and to come right away. The piano had slipped as they were lifting it off the ground. It landed on Tom's shin and his foot. The aftermath of that "little accident" was nearly tragic. Not only did he break his foot, but he had two severe infections that almost cost him his foot. He spent two weeks in the hospital and several months on antibiotics. His foot eventually healed, but he never walked as before and was unable to work full-time the following year.

For the next three years, Tom homeschooled Tommy while I worked full-time. It was then that we really started to see our son soar. We put the accident behind us and focused on educating him.

So here we were, this unique little family of three: Tom in his 60s, I in my late 30s and Tommy six. Life was good. We were comfortable.

Those who follow Christ probably know what comes next, don't you? When we walk with God, we don't stay comfortable for very long. In fact, I've learned that my comfort is my biggest handicap in my Christian walk. Comfort invites complacency. But knowing this doesn't mean that I enjoy discomfort. Who does? We learn to expect it and we can learn to appreciate its value in our lives, but I'll probably never enjoy the disruption of my comfort till I'm whole in Christ.

In the spring of 2010, we were attending an Easter Egg Hunt with our homeschool support group. It was our first such event and we enjoyed the chance to meet many new folks. Little did I know that the conversations I'd have this day would dramatically change the course of my life!

Tom often said of me, "Honey, you sure do have a flair for understatement!" I can hear him saying it again as I write these words. This was no small life change that was about to overtake us!

That day we met Kim, who had adopted two young daughters from China and was in the process of adopting again. Kim was sharing her most recent adoption process, the daughter they were seeking to adopt, and some travel plans she had. It was intriguing, and I listened intently. In an effort to contribute something to the conversation, I shared a comment that Tommy had made to me about six months earlier.

One day, while riding in the van, Tommy piped up from the back seat, "Mom, I think you and Dad should adopt a brother for me!" To me, this little edict had come out of the clear blue sky. Not wanting to discourage him, but having absolutely no intention of adopting a child, I diplomatically explained to Tommy that the Lord gifted some families with many children, and then others, like ours, were meant to have but one child. I told him that he was the perfect child for our family. And that was the end of that. Or so I thought.

After she heard about the conversation, Kim asked, "Didn't you think that was an unusual question for a six-year-old? Don't most boys his age ask their parents for a new baby brother or sister rather than an adopted sibling? Do you know many adoptive families?" These were all good and reasonable questions, to be sure. But Tommy was always saying things that weren't typical, so it didn't make a strong impression on me at the time. I think I said something like, "Well, you'd have to know Tommy. Nothing he says shocks us anymore." But her questions stuck with me and began to make me wonder if indeed there was more to his innocent request.

Before we left that day, Kim said that if we ever felt the Lord calling us to adopt, she'd love to share with us about special needs kids from China. She told me that she and a friend of hers advocated for waiting kids in that country, and that she'd be happy to answer any questions that I might have on the subject. In an effort to get out of that conversational corner, I announced that my husband would never be approved to adopt as he was too old. That's right! I totally used my old man as an excuse! This, I thought, would surely be something she could not refute. I thanked her for her offer and we left that day thinking we had sufficiently put adoption out of our minds.

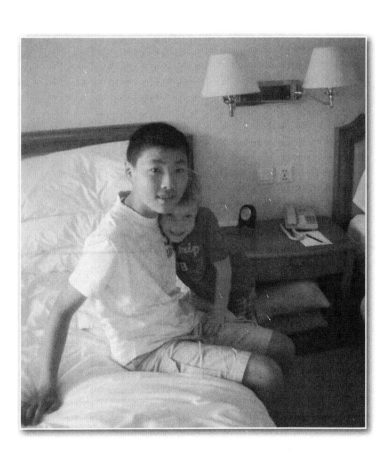

CHAPTER FIVE

Adoption?

❧

*T*ry as I might to dismiss the memory of the conversations that began at the park, over the course
of the next week or so, adoption swirled all around
us. Whether it was new families that we met through
other friends who'd adopted, or a storyline on a popular
TV program, it was everywhere! In fact, the following
Wednesday evening, as we were watching TV, Tom, who
was always multitasking his entertainment, reading and
watching TV simultaneously, put down his book, and
loudly announced that he thinks God was asking us to
adopt.

In case you missed it, this was my sixty-eight-year-
old husband! The same husband who almost ten years
before had said that if I wanted a baby, I'd need to find a
new husband! It may have been one of the few times in
my life that I was legitimately speechless.

When I was able to speak, I asked him what in the world he was thinking! He reminded me of all the ways that adoption had crossed our paths in the previous week and that it was so "in our face" that it just had to be the Lord who was drawing us there. He asked me to contact "that lady from the park" and at least investigate things more. "Ok, what could it hurt?" I thought. If this was just bad burritos and not something coming from the Lord, it would not bear any fruit and we'd once again be off the hook.

To be completely honest, if this suggestion had come from anywhere other than Tom's mouth directly, I would have blown it off as pure madness. God knew, given our history, that Tom would need to be the one to lead this particular effort, or I'd never see it as divinely inspired. Hesitantly, I emailed Kim and she sent me the file of a seven-year-old Chinese boy almost immediately. She walked me through some rudimentary basics of the adoption process and after discussing it with Tom, I called the agency that had this child's file. I was almost relieved, a little, when they promptly told me they would not approve us to adopt this child.

As I had suspected, Tom's age was an issue and furthermore, it was explained that they would not approve an adoption "out of birth order." This particular boy was one year older than our son. Knowing virtually nothing about the adoption process, I assumed these were deal breakers and informed Kim that we could not be approved to adopt, but thanked her for her time.

What happened next changed everything. Kim clarified something that, being a novice to adoption, I'd not understood. She explained the difference between adoption law, country process, and agency preference. As it turned out, what we were told from this agency wasn't the final word on our ability to adopt a child. It was simply that specific agency's policy and standard protocol. She encouraged me to take some time to learn about the waiting child process in China, to pray for direction from the Lord, and to join an online group that advocated for those going through the China Special Needs program.

In a matter of days, I'd joined the group, spent time reading posts and familiarizing myself with the information provided there, and looking at photos of waiting children. Then it happened.

I saw a photo album titled "Aging Out Kids." I opened it and began to research what that term actually meant. As a former Middle School Band Director, having worked with many kids in their early teen years, I was astonished to learn that, in China, children age out, or become ineligible for adoption on their fourteenth birthday. Fourteen! In this folder were the faces of so many boys and girls, all nearing their fourteenth birthdays and the end of their chance at a family to call their own.

I thought about how hard things were for me emotionally at thirteen. I remembered the stress of wanting to measure up, be good enough, be accepted by my peers. Those were tough years for my family financially and at times I felt like "poor white trash." When someone befriended me, I wondered if they genuinely liked me or if they felt pity for me. I could not fathom being at that age and not having a family to lean on. I couldn't wrap my mind around a future like the one these children faced.

God began to work in my own heart and as surprised as I was to realize it, He had a thirteen-year-old from that very folder in mind to join our little family, and soon!

Click. Click. Click. One by one, I clicked past the faces of these children, so many children. Each one a real, valuable person who needed a family. Then, in one click, I saw that face. There on the screen, looking straight into my heart, was a boy in a bright blue fleece with a precious smile. Below his photograph were a couple of sentences about him. I remember lingering on that page, but then clicked on past once more. But I found myself returning to it every few clicks. There was something I couldn't put my finger on. Was it his reported love of Math? Perhaps. Tom had been a Math teacher for over thirty years and this certainly was a neat connection. Was it the vibrant color of his jacket that caught my attention? Maybe. I do love this shade of blue. I mention these less significant details, because honestly, it may have been one or both of those things that God used to draw my attention toward this child. After all, there was little else that I could surmise from this page with such limited information. Later that afternoon, with that face still etched in my mind's eye, I printed off his basic info and walked it downstairs to share it with Tom.

When God began to pull on Tom's heart, and then mine, regarding adoption, it wasn't a teenager's face I saw. My initial image was that of a younger child, maybe five to seven years old. I pictured a playmate and close sibling for Tommy. So, to say that my attraction to this thirteen-year-old boy was somewhat of a shock to me would be a serious understatement. Even Tom was surprised when I handed him that paper and he saw a teen. When he questioned me, all I could say to him was, "Honey, I can't explain it, but I think this is our son."

That day is etched in my mind. It was Good Friday 2011. We knew absolutely nothing about international adoption, and to be honest, if we had, we'd have never started this process. You see, what we didn't know was that back then, adopting a child internationally in four months' time was practically unheard of. When we made those initial agency calls, we were told that it was a potentially impossible situation. You see, the China adoption process does not have a grace period. We would have to complete the adoption process in full before his fourteenth birthday, or he would not be allowed to come home as our son, even if we were in China waiting. I was speaking to a woman named Elizabeth from the placing agency that had our son's file. She was trying her best to paint a realistic picture of our chances, and she told us that if they allowed us to proceed with this adoption, we'd have to know that they could not guarantee successful completion, especially in light of the tight time frame. I'll never forget my response to her. "Elizabeth, I know we are new to adoption, and I want you to know that I hear you, but I'm fairly certain that God has plans for this child and they include being a part of our family."

I had no idea that life as we knew it had just ended. From that point forward, everything else took a back seat to getting this child home. The process was daunting, but we were determined. I won't bore you with the details of the paperwork, and clearances, and political string-pulling of the next four months. Suffice it to say that God moved mountains to orchestrate Colin's journey into our family. Throughout these months, we learned what real community looked like. We had an army of friends, family and local supporters who came alongside us to facilitate fundraisers and to help out with Tommy during those times of intense paper pushing and deadlines. Looking back, I realize that some of my closest friends came into my life during this time and I am doubly blessed.

About halfway through our paper chase for Colin, another boy caught my heart. It was a quiet afternoon, and I was on the computer just minding my own business! I was reading through messages on an adoption group, asking for support and assistance from other in-process families, and there he was. In that same folder of older kids, I saw a boy with the name "Scott." He literally took my breath away. This was, in all honesty, the most beautiful young boy I'd ever seen! I was completely entranced by his face on that screen. I was stunned to learn that he'd been waiting so long for a family.

Since we've already established how little we knew about the adoption process, I naively emailed my agency and asked my caseworker to explain what things might look like if we were to pursue both boys at once. The bottom line came back that if we were to add this second child now, and wait for the appropriate approvals to come through, that we would be putting Colin's adoption at risk because of his impending birthday. I saw this as a clear answer from the Lord that we were not to change course. Tom and I were fully committed to bringing Colin home and could not do anything that might jeopardize that. I prayed that this other child would find a family to call his own and refocused my efforts on our current adoption.

Two more months passed before we would travel to China to adopt Colin. After four months of hard work and prayer, we arrived in China in mid-August 2011, to officially adopt Colin as our son, just seven days before he turned fourteen! We were about to become a family of four.

After a grueling twenty-five hours of travel from Los Angeles, Tom and I stepped off the plane in Shanghai, China with six-year-old Tommy. Though Tom had served in Asia as a helicopter pilot during the Vietnam era, this was my first time abroad. I thought I'd prepared myself, but as we left the plane and walked into the gate area, there was a sign overhead that I could not read. I felt an overwhelming uneasiness with each step, realizing that I couldn't read any of the signs and had no idea where to go. We nervously followed the crowd hoping that they would lead us to customs. I asked Tom if he thought any of the airport staff would speak English. We still had one more flight to catch that would take us to Shenyang, Colin's city.

Adding to the stress of feeling lost in a foreign land, Tommy was getting a lot of attention. Families who had gone before had told us that fair-skinned children, in particular, would likely garner extra attention. Tommy's complexion and white-blond hair certainly caught people's eyes in a sea of ebony. As we shuttled from the tarmac to our gate, I remember wedging little Tommy carefully between us so that no one would touch him. Understandably, our son was tired and a little frightened after our long journey. Our small shuttle bus was packed wall to wall with people with absolutely no personal space concerns.

Everywhere we went in China, people stared at him, and often reached out to touch his face or hair, as if to see if this fair-skinned, blond-haired boy was real. Thankfully, we managed to make our next flight, and we arrived at the airport in Shenyang at around 11 pm local time. After being greeted by a hired car service, and riding another hour into town, we checked into our hotel and crashed, utterly exhausted.

Our first day in Shenyang was Sunday, and much to our surprise, the guide hired by our adoption agency had missed his train from Beijing and would not be able to meet us until the following day. There we were, three Americans with absolutely no knowledge of the Chinese language or culture, alone in the fourth largest city in China. So, where do we go? Wal-Mart, of course! We were blessed to find a hotel staff person who spoke enough English to direct us down the main street about eleven blocks to the closest Wal-Mart where we could get some bottled water and other necessities. On our way there, we eyed a McDonald's as well, so we made plans to head there for dinner. We were not about to venture too far from our hotel without a guide.

If you've ever been to New York City, perhaps you can imagine the intense sensory overload we experienced that day. It is the closest comparison that I can make from personal experience. As we walked down the street, trying not to get lost, but wanting to take in every sight and sound, I was struck by the high-rise buildings. The masses teemed around us on foot; riding mopeds and bicycles; and crowded into cars, taxis and buses. Tom said he couldn't believe that the streets weren't littered with bodies with the way people drove there. Things we use as guidelines here in America, like street signs, traffic lights and lane dividers, were more suggestive than restrictive in China. Men, women, and even children would ride bicycles within inches of a moving car or city bus and it was frightening to watch. It was common to see an entire family riding together on a moped or motorcycle. All around we heard the roar of a collective mob talking on their cell phones, thousands of cars braking, honking and maneuvering for position on the roads.

After what seemed like a long walk, we finally saw the Wal-Mart sign. As we crossed the busy street and headed toward what looked like the front of the store, we were intrigued that even the Wal-Mart was unique in its appearance and functional layout. Because real estate is scarce in China, almost every business has a tiny base footprint, and builds up. The Wal-Mart was no exception. The first thing we noticed was that there was no door. Well, not a traditional door anyway. Covering the entrance of the store were heavy plastic strips, like what you'd see in the entrance to a commercial restaurant cooler. We pushed our way through and began to look around. It is safe to say that nothing but the sign resembled any Wal-Mart we'd ever seen. The produce, along with spices, herbs, and even meats were displayed mainly in open boxes or display cases. We saw critters that we'd never seen nor heard of. Fascinated, I whipped out my camera to capture the scene.

As we crossed the store and turned a corner, we saw a kind of moving sidewalk, only, this one was going to the second floor. We pushed our cart onto the beltway and held on as a steep incline moved us up to another department. This particular Wal-Mart was three stories high, but it was smaller in square footage than a Super Wal-Mart in the States. We quickly learned that the Chinese do not shop as we do. Like many cultures around the world, the Chinese shop for small quantities more often. Many would shop each day after work and prepare the meal from fresh ingredients.

After touring the store, and getting our fix of tourist pictures, we bought our bottled water, only to remember the long walk back to the hotel. Poor Tom carried that heavy case the whole way. That trip provided an opportunity for us to sightsee a bit more now that we knew our way. Street vendors were cooking up some incredible foods that smelled delicious. Large banks and office buildings stood between small stores and restaurants. Every shop had merchandise prominently displayed on the sidewalks and many had employees standing outside calling to passersby about sales to entice them inside. The main difference between this walk and one we might have taken in New York? In Shenyang, as far as the eye could see was a sea of rich, black hair and olive skin. Except us. In the middle of this throng of people were the strange-looking Americans with their porcelain-doll son. You couldn't help notice the stares, the smiles and the whispers. I'd never felt so conspicuous in all my life. Tommy stayed close as we walked along. He didn't seem scared as much as fascinated, but he wasn't about to risk getting lost either, so he held onto my hand tightly. His eyes grew big as he took in all the strange sights and sounds.

Back at the hotel we relaxed and tried to mentally prepare to meet our new son. After a little cajoling, we got Tommy to sleep and Tom and I sat on the bed discussing what the next day might bring. Tom seemed so calm and self-assured. I was very excited to finally be meeting Colin, but at the same time I was nervous. I prayed that God would calm our hearts and prepare us for our new life together.

In the morning our guide met us in the hotel lobby. He explained the basics of what to expect that day, led us to a van, and introduced us to our driver. As we left the hotel, we got to experience firsthand some of that famous Chinese driving we had seen the day before. It was almost better when our eyes were closed. Not only were the drivers insane, but there were no seatbelts in the car, so we squeezed Tommy between us and held on tight.

After parking at the Shenyang Civil Affairs office, we all crossed the street, taking our lives into our hands, then walked up the concrete steps of the large office building. We stopped for a quick picture as the gravity of our circumstance came over me. This would be the last picture we would take as a family of three. My mind flashed back to the years that I'd begged God for a child. Instantly, I was back in that orchestra pit hearing the Lord's promise that I'd one day be a mother. And then, just as quickly, I was back on those steps getting ready to meet my second son. I was so nervous. I was confident that God had brought us here for this purpose, but there were still so many unknowns. Would he be scared? Would he change his mind about letting us adopt him? How would he react to Tommy, and vice versa?

Up we went to the floor that housed the adoption office. As the elevator doors opened, we saw a waiting area full of sofas with a long hallway to the left and to the right. The room opened up to a long counter with several staff desks behind it. Our guide was directing us to the right to check in while my eyes scanned the place frantically for any glimpse of Colin. As we proceeded closer to the check-in counter, out of my right eye, I spotted him. He was sitting in a swivel chair in front of the desk talking to someone in Chinese. He glanced over his left shoulder hearing someone approaching. He seemed to recognize us from the photos we'd sent and he stood to greet us.

As Colin stood up, I was struck that my new son was taller than me! My mind swirled with emotion. I was overwhelmed to see him in the flesh, this boy we'd prayed for and labored to adopt for four months. I wanted him to like us and was nervous about doing or saying the wrong thing. He seemed timid, but not scared. I asked the translator to ask him about a hug. I wanted to respect his personal space. I was, after all, a total stranger, but he consented and allowed both Tom and me to hug him. Can you even imagine Tom Rylands *not* hugging someone he loved? I have never met a more physically demonstrative man in my life. Tom, being raised mostly by women after the death of his father in 1944, was very affectionate and didn't waste an opportunity to demonstrate that with word or deed. Hugging Colin for the first time was like hugging a tree. He was stiff and didn't seem to know what to do, but it felt good to finally wrap my arms around him.

After completing the paperwork and picking up supplies at the store, we settled back at the hotel. Within five minutes, Tommy and Colin were chasing each other all over the room like they'd been brothers all their lives. Tommy would chase Colin and catch him, only to have

Colin turn the tables and chase him back. Then, Colin scooped Tommy up just like his Daddy often did and body slammed him into the hotel bed. Tommy giggled and giggled. He adored his new big brother.

Later our guide met us to escort us to dinner. We decided to walk three blocks away to a small noodle restaurant. There were a whopping three items on the menu. On our walk there, the thing that struck me most was seeing Colin immediately jump to Tommy's left to shield him from traffic. It reminded me of all the times that Tom had done the same for me. He put his arm around Tommy's little shoulder and walked that way all the way to dinner. That's when I knew that this young man was created to be a big brother. It was in his nature to protect others. At that moment, all my fears and suspicions melted away. We were going to be fine.

The typical adoption process in China involves spending about a week in the child's birth province, then a week in Guangzhou in Guangdong province. During week one, after the adoption is finalized, you apply for the child's passport. This process generally takes a few days, so it allows families the opportunity to sightsee and take in the culture of their child's home city. We wanted to see some of the historical sights, and we also asked the guide to take us where we could purchase some authentic souvenirs that were unique to Shenyang. At his suggestion, we went to a local gift shop to purchase small pieces of art made out of bird feathers, a local craft of the indigenous peoples. As we walked up to the second floor of the shop, we were overwhelmed with the reception we received. I had almost forgotten what a spectacle we were until a large group of young Chinese women saw Tommy and began to squeal, loudly! Honestly, the way they were carrying on you'd have thought a famous rock star had just entered the room! They ran over to us, and began to speak to our guide, apparently asking if they could take pictures of Tommy. One by one, about twenty girls squatted down next to our shy six-year-old, and a friend would take their picture. At first, Tommy clung to my leg and hid behind me, but little by little, he warmed up to the idea and agreed to pose for the pictures. The funniest part was when our guide whispered to Tommy, "One dollar, Tommy! Tell them pictures are one dollar!"

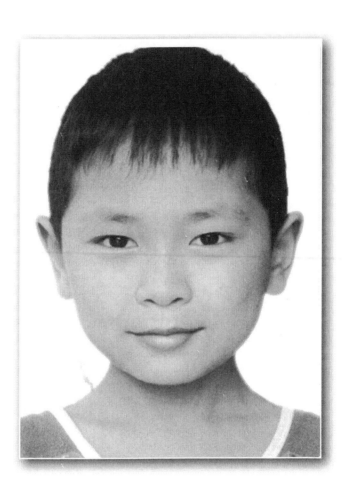

CHAPTER SIX

Back So Soon?

✤

*A*fter a week in Shenyang, we secured Colin's passport and made our way to Guangzhou where we would conduct his visa medical appointment and receive his travel visa for the United States.

We celebrated Colin's fourteenth birthday in Guangzhou before coming home on Labor Day Weekend 2011. Once home, life was hectic and we all worked very hard to help Colin transition well. The massive upheaval in his life is like nothing most people ever experience. This brave young man was now living on the other side of the world with strangers who looked, talked, behaved, and probably even smelled completely foreign to him. Our food, culture and rituals were so different than what he'd been accustomed to. It was a slow process, and a busy one, but he bonded very well with his new family. All things considered, it was easier than we had expected.

You might think that we had little time to think about anything except reshaping our little family, but you'd be wrong.

"Scott" was still on my heart. In fact, he was so heavy on my heart that I teamed up with two friends, Kim (the friend who introduced us to adoption) and my sweet friend Annie, to advocate for him. We were determined to find this precious boy a home. We plastered that pretty face everywhere and shared his need for a home. Our efforts seemed fruitful, as several loving, godly families asked about him and a few even called the agency for more information. Imagine our disappointment when, one by one, these families were turned away. We were baffled. Week by week, his fourteenth birthday inched closer. Week by week, his chances of finding an adoptive family looked more slim. It became obvious that only a family who had previously adopted, who already had a dossier logged in with the authorities in China, would be able to get to him before his birthday. This made the pool of possible families much smaller…as if families willing to adopt an aging out child wasn't already crazy small.

So, here I was, a brand new adoptive parent, a completely novice orphan advocate, determined to find a family for "this boy." I called Kim one day, sharing my emotional pull for this child and I remember telling her that it just wasn't okay for him to age out. I recognized that so many kids do, and said, "I know we can't save them all, but this one, this one cannot age out!" As we continued to brainstorm possible ways to advocate more effectively for him, I thought I'd email the agency, explain our goal to assist with locating a family for him, and ask to see his file. I figured that if I knew everything there was to know about him, I'd be better able to share about his needs and be a more effective advocate. At first, they said no. I was dumbfounded. Did they not understand that his time was running out? Of course, now I understand why they were hesitant to share his file. We were a new adoptive family, home only a few weeks at this point, and she was afraid that I'd want to adopt him myself. They were trying to protect me from even the temptation. I was told quite clearly that no family who had just adopted would ever be approved to adopt again so soon after returning home.

Another week went by, then another. With each week that passed, my heart was more burdened for this boy I just couldn't put out of my mind. A second time, I reached out to the agency asking to see his file, and again they said no. As we got into October, I tried one last time. Finally, due to the extremely tight time frame, they agreed to allow me to see the file. I read about his special needs, his clubbed feet at birth and the circumstances surrounding his coming into government care. As you might imagine, this only made me love him more!

I shared my heart for this child with Tom, who knew that I'd been praying for him and working with Kim and Annie to get him a family. He sympathized over his plight, but was not immediately ready to volunteer to be his parent. Remember, we had been home for mere weeks ourselves and still had some debt from our first adoption. But, as we have learned again and again, God's will often defies common sense or the excuses we put in the way. It was a Wednesday afternoon when I approached Tom one last time about this child. He was standing over a pot of spaghetti before heading out to church for orchestra practice. I hadn't really thought through what it would look like if he actually said yes, but I knew God had connected me with this child for a reason. Much to my surprise, Tom said yes. He said yes! He didn't even turn from the spaghetti to look at me. He just said yes!

I raced to the phone to call the agency rep I'd been conversing with for several weeks. I asked her if they would consider allowing us to adopt "Scott." I was fully expecting a speech about bonding and the importance of focusing on Colin during this time. And I knew it was important and that I couldn't argue the point. She did not disappoint. But, what came after that was truly incredible. She told me that as a matter of policy, they would not be able to approve us, but that she was willing, in light of "Scott's" impending birthday, to at least make a request to their governing board to consider us as a possible match. I thought, "That's all I can ask" and I thanked her for her time.

Once off the phone, I told Tom what had happened and I told him I didn't expect that we'd hear of their decision for at least a week, not knowing how often their board met to discuss such matters. We finished dinner and hopped in the car to head to church. As I shut the door, my phone rang. I was in shock to hear the adoption agent's voice on the other end. It hadn't even been an hour since I'd spoken with her! She began by telling me how unusual this was, but said that if we could get our local social worker on board and in support of this plan, they were willing to allow us to apply as his new parents. After all the times that God made me wait for an answered prayer, these times of immediate response totally made up for them!

The first call I made was to Kim. I will never forget this phone call as long as I live. I told her our news and then, almost like a sudden shower, fear crept into my heart. I thought about all the work that we'd completed for Colin's adoption and all of the cost, and the debt we still had to pay off for our last trip and….. Then Kim said, "Angie, I know that God clearly orchestrated Colin's adoption, but you worked your butt off to make that happen! Something tells me, He just isn't going to let you take any credit for this one!" Boy, was she right! The miracles that we witnessed during the next eight weeks were astonishing. You read that right. Eight weeks. From the time we submitted our official letter of intent (the letter to the Chinese government asking permission to adopt a specific child) till the time we met him face to face was eight short weeks! And we thought our last adoption set records!

Clearly, that quiet afternoon in front of the computer, that day I first saw his face, was one that God Himself set in motion, knowing that in His perfect time, our second adopted son, whom we named Cameron, would join our family. I am still humbled when I think about the intimate way in which our heavenly Father orders our steps. One of the greatest privileges of my life has been teaching and illustrating this truth to our sons. For them to know that even in their darkest and saddest days, God saw *them*. He still sees them. Each of our boys has a unique story. Their journey home to our family is personal and special and divinely crafted by God.

Beginning another adoption process in October put us on the fastest track to our son that you could imagine. It also meant that we would be traveling back to China in December. Traveling that far is a physically taxing affair, especially in coach seating, so Tom, who had suffered with a degenerative back condition for many years, decided that it was best all around for him to wait at home this time. Tom stayed home with Tommy and I took Colin to serve as translator and to help put Cameron at ease. As we got closer to receiving our travel approval, it was looking as if we'd need to fly out right before Christmas. This was an extremely expensive proposition. Traveling around a major world holiday made for higher airfares and we were trusting God each day for the funding required just to pay our way through the various fee deadlines. So we began to brainstorm ways to reduce expenses.

I remember being at my mother's farm in South Carolina that Thanksgiving. By this time, I'd gotten into the habit of checking airfares almost every day to spot trends for December travel. It was becoming clear that if we didn't leave the United States by the tenth of December, our travel expenses would almost double.

From the farm, I called our caseworker and asked her about traveling early. I began this conversation by acknowledging that I knew she couldn't *recommend* what I was about to suggest. I knew that she couldn't guarantee anything with regard to our timed approvals for travel. I continued to explain that if we didn't leave earlier than projected, that we might not make it at all. Therefore, I posed the question, "If we were to get on a plane and travel to China on December 6th, without yet receiving our formal travel approval, would you do everything in your power to get it in time for us to adopt Cameron by December 12th?" She replied with a yes, though there were several caveats attached. That was all I needed to hear.

Colin and I boarded a non-stop flight from Dulles to Beijing on December 6, 2011. I contacted a popular guide service (run by an adoptive mother I'd met along the way) and arranged for her to pick us up in Beijing, make hotel reservations for four days, and book our flight from Beijing to Wuhan the following Sunday. What our agency wanted an additional $2200 to arrange for us, she handled for less than $750! I explained our financial situation and told her that I did not require bells and whistles, but that if at all possible, could she please arrange for Colin and me to see the Great Wall of China? It was the one thing that I felt he must see if we were going to Beijing. Not only did she agree, but she booked us in a small, inexpensive hotel within walking distance of Tiananmen Square, the Forbidden City, and other popular attractions. Unlike our trip to China in August, it was now December and it was cold! The days we spent awaiting our travel approval documents were quite brisk, but we were also blessed with an unusual break from the smog. We had a bright blue sky and the sun shone in all its glory. Colin and I walked the better part of one afternoon taking in the local sights and sounds and it didn't cost us a penny.

Friday was the day we joined the tour group heading to the Great Wall. Colin, though he was born in China, had never seen the Wall and I was thrilled to see it as well. I've mentioned the traffic in China before and believe me, Beijing was no better! What should have taken us an hour took almost three. When we arrived at the entrance to the Great Wall, we moved up as a group to the chair lifts that would take us to the top of the Wall. Colin looked white as a ghost as we ascended, but when asked, he was quick to tell me he wasn't scared. Typical teenager!

When we arrived at the top, the view was breathtaking. This massive structure — built by hand — was a remarkable thing to ponder. The stone steps were shallow and steep. We were at a higher elevation than we'd been back in town and there was snow and ice on the steps. We had to tread the slippery steps carefully. Colin was like a grasshopper. He ran on ahead of me and made every stride look effortless. Thankfully, I wasn't the only adult who lagged behind a bit. This climb was not for the faint of heart, but eventually, I made it to the top. From there, not only could we look out over a vast wooded area of land with its own unique beauty, but we could also see a long stretch of the very wall we'd just climbed. It curved across the horizon like a beautiful stone snake cutting through the mountains. It was obvious to me why it is regarded as one of the world's greatest wonders. Sharing this experience with Colin is a memory I will always cherish.

Our drive back to Beijing was even slower than our trek out had been: four hours. Knowing we would not make our intended next activity, our guide searched out a public restroom for a quick pit stop. Now, I'm not a big believer in coincidence and this was Friday, the last business day of the week. And did I mention that we still hadn't received our travel approval from the Chinese authorities yet? Well, as it happened, the public restroom we visited was directly across the street from the CCCWA (China Center for Children's Welfare and Adoption) building in Beijing, where all adoption approvals are processed. RIGHT ACROSS THE STREET! Our guide casually mentioned it as we walked along the sidewalk. I asked her if there was any way that I could go over there and inquire about my approval, but she said no. The travel approval documents had to be delivered through proper channels in order to be valid. In this case, that meant overnight mail to Wuhan. I knew then that if those papers weren't mailed in the next hour, they would not make it to the Civil Affairs office in Wuhan in time for our Monday morning adoption appointment. I couldn't believe that I was standing right outside the office and there was nothing I could do. It was out of my hands.

On Sunday, we boarded our flight to Wuhan, settled into our hotel, and met our new adoption guide. We tried to relax, though that is often impossible the night before you meet your new child. We went to the store to buy some fruit and other snacks to have on hand and skyped home to talk to Tom and Tommy.

Monday morning came and our appointment time at Civil Affairs was ten o'clock. Our driver dropped us off and our guide led us through a small lobby to the elevator. My stomach was in knots. As we stepped off the elevator, we entered a small hallway and then proceeded into a waiting room with some sofas and toddler toys along the perimeter. We stood fidgeting as our guide sought out the Director for further instructions. We had arrived before Cameron and his chaperone. As we waited, I remember worrying that our approval hadn't arrived on time and that we would not be allowed to take Cameron with us. We knew when we chose to leave the States early that this was a possibility.

The Director's office was surrounded by glass and I could see them talking inside. Boy how I wanted to know what they were saying. A few moments later, our guide came out to tell me that our travel approval had arrived just an hour before we had. I was so relieved! With that very important detail taken care of, we could turn our attention to the son we were about to meet.

Within minutes, in walked the most precious little fellow escorted by a female chaperone. He was wearing a bright turquoise winter jacket and they walked over toward us and introductions were made. We knew that he probably wasn't almost fourteen, like his paperwork indicated, but I will admit that I was a bit shocked at his petite stature. He was still the most beautiful boy, but small, probably closer to ten than fourteen. We took our official picture together for the government and signed the obligatory paperwork. Knowing a bit better what to expect than I had the first time in China, I was ready to get fees paid and documents signed so that we could get to the store, let Cameron pick out some snacks, and get him settled in with us at the hotel.

One of the first things you do when meeting your child is to determine if you planned well. Did you bring him the right size clothes? Have you prepared properly for his needs? In Cameron's case, even though we expected him to be a smaller boy, we still overshot a bit. As I had him change his clothes, I was shocked that he'd been sent to us with not one, not two, but three pairs of pants on. Once we peeled off all those layers, our little guy needed a size 8 pant instead of a size 10. Thankfully, we always buy jeans with an adjustable waist! The next few days were spent with Colin translating between Cameron and me and the three of us getting acquainted.

CHAPTER SEVEN

Meeting God in China

❦

A few weeks before we went to China to adopt Cameron, I lost my job. It really threw me for a loop. Of course our surprises aren't surprises to the Lord; He knew precisely what He was doing. He also knew I wouldn't be able to search for a new job until after my return. Who would hire someone who announces they'll be taking a month off work in a few weeks? So, in some ways, that took a little pressure off.

On this, my second trip to China in less than five months, I had a truly holy encounter with the Lord. We were in our hotel room in Guangzhou. I had just gotten the boys to bed and was taking some time to finish reading *Crazy Love* by Francis Chan. As I finished the book, I felt the strong presence of the Lord and I turned my head toward the sleeping boys a few feet away. Again, as happened many years before, He spoke clearly to my spirit and said, "This isn't just about them." I wasn't quite sure, at first, if I'd heard that correctly. Pondering this for awhile and praying about it that night, I felt that it had something to do with a career decision, but hadn't the faintest idea what.

The next morning, I skyped with Kim and shared that I felt the Lord leading me to something work-related, but I had no idea what. I asked her to commit to pray with and for me. She agreed and for the next week or so, she did just that. Upon returning home, Christmas Eve, 2011, I scheduled a time for a small group of adoptive moms to stop over for coffee and prayer. We had enjoyed this routine for over a year and we'd missed our time together since my trip and the holidays. As the children played outside, I gathered these ladies around the kitchen table and shared with them my experience in the hotel room. Again, I asked these women of faith to pray about this with me. I was actively seeking clarity and direction from the Lord. It was around that very table that the Lord began to reveal His plan.

Kim suggested that with my administrative bent, and newfound passion for orphan care and adoption, perhaps I should consider opening an adoption agency. The idea seemed to make some sense and I did think about it for a while, but the confirmation never came. As we discussed the trends we were seeing in our own community and the increase in adoptions, someone mentioned the fact that we did not have a solid Christian agency in our area. My own experience to that point had been with two placement agencies from the West Coast, so I had little experience with South Carolina agencies, and the ones I'd hired for our home studies were not gospel-focused. As our conversation deepened, several ladies mentioned Lifeline Children's Services. I had never heard of them, but as I listened, it seemed that their reputation was solid and that the heart of that agency was the gospel above all else. My sweet friend Annie, who'd been actively engaged in orphan advocacy for years, shared several positive interactions that she'd had with Lifeline over that time. We joked about asking them to consider opening an office here in South Carolina. I knew no one at Lifeline, but Annie mentioned some communication she'd had about a year earlier with their International Adoption Director, Dave Wood. So, on what seemed like a total whim, she agreed to email him and see what he thought of our little idea.

Now before you conjure up images of me as this amazing woman of faith, let me take a moment to be transparent. I was perfectly fine with Annie sending this arbitrary email to an agency based in Alabama, but don't think for a second that I saw this as a message from the Lord. In all honesty, at the time, I had visions of our message going straight into the recycle bin! Never in a million years did I think that someone from this national nonprofit would read, much less respond to, an email from two random moms in South Carolina. Boy, was I wrong!

You see, sometimes God's plan isn't contingent upon our faith or agreement. Sometimes He blows our socks off even when we doubt Him. This was such a case. To properly set the stage here, we were in the first week of January when the initial email was sent. Within 24 hours, Annie and I received a reply from Dave. Then another from the Executive Director, Herbie Newell. Gulp!

I vividly recall the morning I got the email from Herbie. He told us that the Board of Directors at Lifeline had, six months earlier, voted to approve an office in South Carolina. He said that, despite the decision to approve this plan, the Board gave clear instructions that they were not to move forward until the Lord clearly opened the door. When I read that, I stopped sipping my coffee and called into the other room to Tom, "Honey, you have to come read this! You aren't going to believe it!" Annie's email, the one I didn't think would even get read, was used by God as the confirmation for these men that the time for a South Carolina office had come!

They indicated an interest in talking with us. Annie, who is my favorite "behind the scenes gal pal," directed their attention to me, and before I knew it, we scheduled an online meeting. The meeting was very productive and within 45 minutes, they'd decided to fly to South

Carolina to discuss the possibilities. When the Lord says move, those mountains move immediately!

In mid-February, Herbie and Dave flew to South Carolina and we met in person. They spent three days meeting with everyone from social workers to adoptive families, lawyers to pregnancy center leaders. Within a few days, both Annie and I were offered jobs. Annie would work alongside the Lifeline China Adoption Team as a part-time Orphan Advocate (her passion) and I would lead the South Carolina office as Director and work through the state licensing process. It was a very exciting time and the start of the most fulfilling ministry work of my life outside of the privilege of parenting our children.

CHAPTER EIGHT

Here We Grow Again

❧

Wrapped in
*W*hen I started to work in orphan care ministry, having now adopted twice, folks teased me that I'd be wanting to bring home every child that touched my heart. Well, I do love each one and hope the best for their futures, but thankfully, I'm not quite *that* tender-hearted. Tom at least was thankful for that. I did, however, often show him the faces of children for whom we were advocating. It was not at all unusual for me to say, "Hey, hon, come take a look at this precious boy!" While this was a common occurrence, it had never resulted in another adoption.

One day in April 2012, I was reading through some adoption-related blogs and I came across one from a long-distance Facebook friend. She was advocating for a young boy in Changsha. He was absolutely adorable! Like so many times before, I called Tom over to look at this precious child. And like so many times before, he commented about the cuteness and went back to his crossword puzzle.

There was something different though. I felt a small sense of disappointment when he walked away, as if I were hoping for some stronger reaction. Just then, he called back over his shoulder, "Hey, hon, you should send his picture to Krisha." Krisha is Tom's eldest daughter, who lives in Virginia with her husband and their two amazing sons. As I contemplated doing just that, it hit me. I can't send this child's photo to her. He's *my* son.

And there I was, again. Looking straight into the eyes of my child on that computer screen. I knew that feeling all too well and I knew that we were there again. I went to Tom and explained why I was not able to email his photo to Krisha, just as I've explained it here. He knew that I had a strong connection to this child and what little bit I'd learned about him, so he consented to request his file and learn more. I immediately emailed our China Program Director at Lifeline and asked her to pull this child's file from the shared list. We reviewed information about his special medical needs and his other personality traits, messaged back and forth with a family who'd met him in person on their own adoption trip, and prayed. It didn't take long this time for both Tom and me to come to a decision.

Though we were surprised to be on this roller coaster again, we were sure that it was God's plan for this boy to be a Rylands. That is the story of our Cooper and how we were first drawn to him. We dove headfirst into the paper chase again, only this time things would look much different. You see, Cooper was only nine years old. Our previous two adoptions had been with boys who, at least on paper, were about to turn fourteen, so each was incredibly expedited and stressful. This adoption would proceed the *normal* way, which was not normal for us! It would be eleven months before we would meet this precious boy in person.

During that time, we filled out form after form, did all the background checks and fingerprints again, applied for adoption grants and raised funds. Yes, there was lots of fundraising to be done in order to cover the expenses of international adoption. In fact, over the course of two and a half years, the Lord helped us raise roughly $100,000 to bring our children into our family. In our economy, that's a very daunting number, but in God's economy, that's equal to us saying yes four times. That's right, *four* times.

You see, about halfway through our journey to Cooper, there was another boy that eked his way into our conversations. Is this sounding familiar to any of you? My friend Kim, who introduced us to adoption in the first place, was very attracted to an older boy from

Chongqing. When she realized that the Lord was not confirming him for her own family, she began to advocate for him as we had for Cameron the year before. I agreed to help, so she sent me his photo and info. One Friday night, just before Tom called us to dinner, I had his info up on my laptop and left it there as I went to eat. As our oldest, Colin, was coming to the table, he noticed the face on my screen and asked me about him. Colin always noticed the faces of older Chinese boys. He wondered if it was a child being adopted into our community. I quickly explained that Ms. Kim and I would be working to get him a family. After dinner, I was scheduled to go with Colin to his first high school football game. Being outdoors sitting on hard metal bleachers for hours on end was Tom's idea of torture, so I won the coin toss on this one. Tommy and Cameron joined us and off we went.

As we headed to the game, Colin asked, "Why don't we just adopt him too?" I explained to him, and to the other boys now listening intently, that the decision to adopt each of them was one that was considered and prayed over carefully. I went on to explain that each time a new member enters a family, the family's limited resources had to stretch a little further and the rest of the family had to be willing to make sacrifices for the good of all.

Then it happened! That beautiful, caring boy, the boy who just one short year ago was the waiting boy around the world, looked over at me and said, "That's true, Mom, but we would only have to give up a little, and he would get everything!"

This fifteen-year-old boy, who now had more than he had ever had, was willing, with virtually no hesitation, to give up the chance at more because he knew what it would mean for someone else.

What does one say to that? Is there any amount of selfishness that can exist in the face of that pure giving spirit? Nothing meant more to me than what we had the opportunity to offer this child.

At this point I was gripping the steering wheel trying not to run off the road. Sometimes, the wisdom of your children will leave you speechless. Hearing my once-orphaned son tell me that our sacrifices would be minimal compared to the gain of family for another son was incredibly humbling. Who knew that truth better than he did?

Later that night, Colin was headed upstairs to bed when he stopped halfway and whispered down to me, "Mom, talk to Dad!" Of course, those who know Colin know that when I say whisper, I do not mean quietly! Colin has often been compared to a "bull in a China shop." Subtlety is not his strength. So, of course, Tom heard what he said.

Once Colin was out of sight, Tom asked what that was all about. I simply said that Colin wanted me to talk to him about "Chad," the name given to this boy for advocacy purposes. He looked surprised, but I did not go any further.

I went to bed that night and was very restless. So, I prayed that if God was intending for us to be doing something with all this, He would show Tom because I was resolute that I was not going to pressure Tom into a fourth adoption. This was going to have to be a clear calling from God.

The next morning Tom was up early cooking a wonderful breakfast for the kids and me (not uncommon for this incredibly spoiled wife). For some strange reason, the boys raced through their food and rushed off to start their chores, leaving Tom and me alone at the table with our coffee. A side note here: this never happens! Did you catch that we were *alone*?

Suddenly, Tom says, "Tell me more about your conversation with Colin last night."

So, I shared with him our conversation in the car. Then, Tom began to say some of the same things that Colin had said the night before. Before I knew it, statements like, "If we brought home another boy...it would mean..." turned into "When we bring him home, we will need to..."

Realizing that the tide had suddenly turned, I asked him, "Do you hear yourself? Are you actually considering this?"

"This child looks like a Rylands," he replied, "and I believe God wants us to bring him home."

Isn't God good? We agreed together that this was our son and called the boys down to discuss it with them. We had an immediate consensus, so we sent off the email to lock his file. From October 2012 through March 2013 when we traveled to China, we were racing ahead for not one child, but two.

CHAPTER NINE

A Search for Faith

❧

*M*y first year at Lifeline was busy. Tom was teaching part-time at a local college, and I was working full-time and then some. This rewarding work made me feel as if I had a prime seat on the 50-yard line of the biggest game of the year. Seeing God bring children into families was incredible. Never before had my work allowed me to feel as if I had such a part in spreading the gospel.

The boys were beginning to bond and we were settling into a somewhat stable routine. A big part of that routine was nightly devotional times with the boys. It was important that we be intentional about sharing our faith with the kids. We shared Bible stories and helped them memorize verses. Tommy, our youngest, had asked to receive Christ into his life during VBS one summer, before God expanded our family through adoption.

Cameron was the first of our new boys to express a desire to invite Jesus into his heart. It was a celebratory event, to be sure, but we weren't solidly convinced that he wasn't just trying to please us. He was slower to give over his life, but eventually, we did see a real change in his heart.

Cooper is our tender heart. He was the most receptive to the gospel and accepted Christ with his Dad and me within six months of entering our family. He was eager to learn more and has been the child who is constantly reminding me of all that God has done to bless us. Whenever I seem sad, it is Cooper who will find me, lay his soft little hand on mine and remind me that I don't have to worry because God is in control. He is the embodiment of childlike faith.

In November of 2013, our three youngest boys celebrated in baptism together at our church. One by one they professed their understanding of the sacrifice that was made on their behalf and their personal desire to serve the Lord.

I'll never forget the night the following spring that Tom called me from a table at a local restaurant. It was a Tuesday and he'd taken Connor with him to teach at the college that night so he could squeeze in an orthodontist appointment that afternoon without having to return home in between. They were getting a quick bite to eat before class started and just as Tom was sitting down to the table, Connor looked up and said, "Dad, I want to have Jesus in my heart." Of course, my husband, who calls himself an absolute emotional slob, began to cry for joy. He prayed with Connor and promptly dialed my number. When I answered, he told me that Connor had some news to share. Connor got on the phone and told me that he was a Christian now. No matter how often you hear those words, especially from your own children, they never lose their wonder. To hear that the Holy Spirit had captured the heart of this child made me giddy with joy. Of all of our boys, he had been the most resistant and hostile to our faith. What made this call even better was when he told me not to tell his brothers because he wanted to be the one to tell them! The next night Connor stood up after dinner, and announced that He believed in God. Cooper cheered and everyone welcomed our new brother into the faith.

Colin, our social butterfly, loved going to church because there were so many other kids there, but to my dismay, he was not interested in spiritual instruction. In his first year in our family, we explained our faith and encouraged Colin to ask questions if he was confused. He often told us that he did not believe these things and that no one in China did either. Tom and I told him that we had a responsibility to teach him about our faith, but that only he could decide what he would believe. We made it clear that he should not do anything just to please us, but only if he wanted to follow Christ. He was very respectful of our faith, but struggled with so many theological issues. Watching my son wrestle spiritually was tough. I told friends that I had never experienced anything like Colin's faith journey. I could almost see the war for his soul.

Month after month, year after year, Colin asked questions of everyone. He asked me, his Dad and any number of pastors. We would try to help him settle those questions but still he wasn't ready. Until he was. And that is how it is, isn't it? We pray for our children to see the truth of the gospel. We teach and we model and we pray some more. And one day, in God's perfect timing, they see their true need for a Savior and choose Christ.

For Colin, it happened one Wednesday night at a church meeting. Tom was at church for orchestra practice and Colin was across the street attending a youth service at another church. Tom had had a long, tiring day and had given Colin specific instructions about being outside at a certain time so that Tom would not have to wait for him.

You can imagine his frustration when he pulled up at the appointed time and Colin was nowhere to be found. I was not there and only got this story secondhand. I could tell Tom wasn't happy. When I asked why, he told me that despite asking for Colin to be on time, he wasn't. So Tom had to enter this large church with hundreds of teens and go looking for him. Let's just say that Colin didn't stand a chance of defending himself in the moment.

As Tom finished his story, I looked across the kitchen at a very frustrated Colin and saw him lay a zipper pouch on the counter. This wasn't just any pouch. On the top of the little bag were large blue letters that said, "I HAVE DECIDED." I could hardly believe what I was reading. I swung around trying to get Tom's attention as he was winding down his rant.

As Colin later explained, during the call to prayer in that night's service, he realized for the first time that he was not going to be able to do all the things that were in his heart without God's help. He finally saw his need for a Savior. While Tom was looking all over for him, Colin was with a pastor sharing his decision. Yes, the night our son accepted Christ as Lord of his life, he got chewed out for being late. Not exactly the hallmark moment this Mom had hoped for, but at the end of the day, we were able to sit with our son, this incredible child that we'd discipled for almost four years, and call him brother. We celebrated his decision and we knew without a doubt that God had captured his heart. He was the last of our children to make our faith his own.

About a month later, our oldest two boys were baptized in the Atlantic Ocean. On this particular June afternoon, the sun was shining bright on the beach, but it was terribly windy. So windy, in fact, that the lifeguards advised that the pastor not go out very deep for the baptisms. In spite of the choppy waves, it was a perfect summer day in Charleston. We were blessed by so many friends and family who came out to support the boys as they made this public profession of their faith. As they were called out into the water, the pastor waved Tom in and asked him to help baptize his sons. What an unexpected privilege! Tom was overwhelmed with gratitude for the opportunity to take part. Our pictures of this special day are among our greatest treasures.

I am often asked about our adoption journey and specifically about how we shared our faith with our sons who joined our family later in their lives. For most Christian families walking the adoption road, their faith is usually what prompted their decision to adopt and is an incredibly important aspect of their family life. They have a strong desire to disciple their new children in the ways of the Lord, but worry, especially in the case of older adoptees, how the gospel will be received. As someone who has been guilty of incorrect thinking myself, let me encourage you in this. You will never convert your child's heart. Only the Holy Spirit can call a lost soul to faith. What you can do—what you must do if you are a Christ-follower—is to teach and model Christ to your children. That is all. Explain to your kids that it is your solemn responsibility as their parents to teach them what you know about faith in God, then live it out. Let yourself off the hook because if you are doing those two things, the results are up to God. I remember how anxious I was about Colin, our first adopted son, and the fact that nothing we said seemed to make a real impact on him. But one day the Holy Spirit gently reminded me that I was not responsible for Colin's choices and that I needed to relax and trust God. From then on, I prayed for him regularly but left the stress of his decision where it belonged: at the cross.

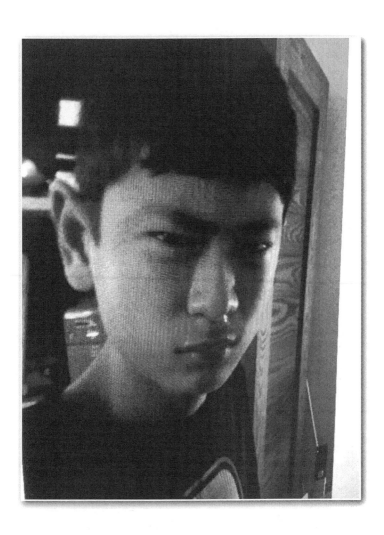

CHAPTER TEN

Adoptive Parenting in the Trenches

*A*doptive and foster parents are a unique breed. We all have individual gifts and talents as well as our own blind spots, but most of these families I've had the honor to know these past few years share a special kind of determination. Invariably, those who choose to parent children with hard beginnings, children so often entering their family with large gaps in their backgrounds, are taking on a kind of messiness that your average family rarely knows. They are choosing to sacrifice their tidy life for one full of uncertainties and heartache.

For a child who has not had the blessing of constant love and appropriate care, there are going to be hard times. It is not a question of if, but rather what, and when, and for how long! Parents who are successful in the world of adoptive parenting are those who are stubborn enough to love this child *no matter what*! That is easier said than done. It is the same kind of love required to stay committed to an unsatisfying marriage or one where only one spouse is putting forth effort.

Having worked with so many adoptive families, and having my own experience with our boys, I can say that not every family struggles in the same way, or to the same degree. In fact, just a few chapters ago, didn't I describe our first adoption as relatively "easy"? Those early months were easy in so many ways. God truly blessed our family when bringing Colin to us; the same is true of each of our sons. But parenting our children carried with it the sober responsibility of meeting them where they were and providing exactly what they needed. The hardest part? Each of our sons had very, very different needs and the needs could change hour by hour. At times I have described my kids as "Jekyll and Hyde," meaning that their moods and their resulting needs would shift on a dime and I had to keep up! It was mentally and physically exhausting.

Without sacrificing their privacy, let me share some things we've faced as adoptive parents. Two weeks after one of our boys came home, another very young child playfully did something that sent our son into a rage that required him to be forcibly restrained. The younger child threw a bucket full of fire pit ash all over our son's head. His eyes were the only distinguishable part of his face. To see the rage and shame and pain up close broke my heart into a thousand pieces. He was completely unable to process his emotions in a healthy way; no one had ever taught him how. Here he was, without the language skills or the emotional skills to express what was in his head and heart, and he simply lost it.

As the young boy's mom and I were inside chatting, we heard an awful scream from the front yard and came running! It took a moment to process what we were seeing. There was my son, chasing this younger friend as if he was out for blood. Right on his heels was our oldest son, chasing after him to protect the little guy from what was sure to be an ugly display of rage if he were caught. Colin did catch his brother in the nick of time and forcibly restrained him as he thrashed around like a dying fish to get free. I thank God that Colin had the quick reaction time and the clarity of mind to jump in, and I shudder to think what the outcome might have been otherwise.

It took us over an hour to calm our enraged son enough to listen to anything his big brother had to say. I felt completely useless since he didn't yet understand any English. I struggled with how to communicate to him that what had happened to him was wrong, and that I understood his anger, but that hurting the younger boy was not okay. Thankfully, God provided a translator who came over that evening so we could talk through this awful incident and try to gain some understanding.

Another son took nearly a year before acting like he belonged in our home. It was like having a boarder renting space from us. His emotional fences were high, as if he was saying, "If I don't care about you, you can't hurt me." This was a stark contrast to the easier transitions that we experienced with some of our other boys. One day after school, he was brooding on the front porch and I decided to join him and see if I could draw him out. When I asked him what was on his mind, he replied that I wouldn't want to know. When I didn't drop it, he finally admitted that he never wanted to be adopted. Ouch.

Tom and I had decided early in our adoption journey that the hard stuff was better let out than stuffed in, so we encouraged our boys to get it out. No matter how hard it was to hear their negative thoughts and feelings, we knew we couldn't fight an enemy we couldn't identify. As a result, we have heard, "I hate you," "I hate America," "I didn't want you," "I don't need you" and "I liked my life better in the orphanage."

The mighty Holy Spirit gave me love instead of defensiveness in those heated situations. He was right there literally speaking through me. I did not utter the words that my flesh wanted to say. Instead, I said, "It's okay. We love you. We will always love you." Ask anyone who knows me; that is not what Angie would have said. No, Angie would likely have said what most parents would have thought in that moment. "How dare you? You ungrateful boy! Don't you know what we had to go through to bring you into this family? Don't you know how *lucky* you are?" But God is constantly saving me…from myself. I'm grateful that He never leaves me, or those I love, without His Holy Spirit. The truth is, these boys aren't lucky. They are blessed, as are we, but their paths in life have been far from lucky. The fact that they needed to be adopted speaks to the brokenness of their world and the pain and suffering of abandonment, neglect and abuse.

Additionally, we have had to navigate lying, jealousy, fighting and other fruits of brokenness and sin. I could write a separate book on our parenting challenges, but I'll summarize by saying that through it all, our goal was to meet those emotional needs and develop a real connection with each boy. We have clung to the truths of Scripture in new ways. I have seen God pour out love on our sons, all of them, in ways that they could not ignore. From the moment of their births, He was drawing them to Himself. Not long after each son entered our family, Tom told them about the Lord and how His hand has been over their lives from day one. He shared with them about God's sovereign plans and how we can trust those plans even when we can't see what He's up to. He would later have this same talk with them about a much harder reality.

So now that I've painted such a picture of older child adoption, why would anyone purposefully choose this life? Oh, dear ones, it is because this life, this choice, has allowed us the biggest honor of our lives! To love, teach, disciple and intercede for these precious souls has allowed us to see God Almighty before our very eyes. To watch the Holy Spirit go to battle for the souls of these boys has humbled me to my knees. To watch the walls come down, to see their hearts healing, to see their eyes begin to open to the truth of God's Word, well, it doesn't get any better than that! God gave us that gift and all we really did was say yes and dig in. He did the heavy lifting. If He is calling your family to stand in the gap for a child in need, He will do the same for you, and abundantly more.

CHAPTER ELEVEN

Healing and Redemption

❦

*N*ow that I've described some of the challenges of adoptive parenting, I'd like to share the other side. You see, this is why you endure the hard times. It's all for the privilege of seeing your child begin to heal. The incredible redemption takes place, sometimes right before your eyes.

Children coming from institutional settings often arrive with some very unflattering behaviors. Maybe they feel the need to fight in order to get your attention. Maybe they aggressively resist your authority because they are afraid of becoming dependent on someone. Perhaps they struggle with anger or shame which presents itself in ways that can be hard to handle. Knowing that this is normal might be helpful on an intellectual level, but day to day, it really doesn't make your home life easier. For our family, the first year of each child coming home was a ton of work. It was hard on all of us, including first and foremost, the newest child. Our challenges paled in comparison to what our new son had to face. And, our sons lacked the tools to deal with all the emotions and realities, because they had not been taught those things. Over the years, we've employed many different parenting and shepherding strategies with our boys because frankly, with their diverse backgrounds, a "one size fits all" approach could have been catastrophic for us all. Parenting these boys the way we'd parented Tommy would not have worked. Their needs were vastly different.

Before going to China to bring Colin home, Tom and I sat Tommy down and explained that his new brother might not know how to act in a family and that he might do or say things that Tommy knew to be wrong or inappropriate. We wanted him to understand this so that he wasn't shocked or scared, but also so that he wouldn't wonder why this kid was "allowed" to act that way. We explained that it would take time for us to gel as a family. We also helped him understand that there may be some times when it seemed that big brother was getting away with things that Tommy never could. We told him that if that ever happened that we needed him to trust us and know that we were handling it in the best way we knew how. As I mentioned, Colin was a very well-behaved child from the beginning, so we didn't really encounter these issues the first time around, but it was important that we all be prepared for it, just in case.

You see, these kids didn't magically appear in our family. They were brought here by God. And the Father who orchestrated their journeys home did not abandon them at the doorstep. He was there with them every step of the way, and mercifully with us as well.

With our boys, the healing started with the little things. Maybe they unintentionally laughed at something that we said, or lingered for a second as we hugged them. Perhaps they agreed to play a board game instead of brooding in their bedroom during family time. These are examples of the baby steps that our boys took toward a brighter future. As time went on, we began to see them come to us with a private need, or open up a tiny crack in the defensive wall and share some small, insignificant detail from their past. All of these were small signs of growth and acceptance. For some, the healing started shortly after their adoptions and for others it took months upon months for them to begin to soften to the idea of being a Rylands boy.

One of the greatest parenting decisions we ever made was the day I finally caved and we adopted our dog, Missy. I didn't grow up with pets, so I didn't have a clue how therapeutic a pet could be. When I saw our toughest boy soften around that dog, I was blown away! She showed him a love that broke through all of his defenses and he grew incredibly close to her. In fact all the boys did. Tom had wanted a dog for ages and I just wasn't ready to take on that added expense and responsibility. If I had known then what I know now, I'd have gotten that dog years earlier. Missy is our "best girl" and though she has grown closest to Connor, all the boys love her dearly.

Before we knew it, the child who had the shortest trigger of all, took ten minutes to calm down after an episode of anger rather than forty-five. That was progress. He was learning how to rein in his emotions. He was learning that our home was a safe place to blow it and that he could turn things around himself.

Most importantly, through the work of the Holy Spirit and some intentional discipling, our boys slowly opened their hearts to the truth of the gospel. Having grown up in church and accepted Christ as a young child, I was amazed to see what an incredible difference there was in our sons when the work of God began to take root in their hearts.

One day, we were all in a large discount store and I was looking through the book section. Tommy was nagging me incessantly for a comic book. I told him I wasn't going to buy it, but he continued to beg me for it. Before I could respond a second time, one of our older boys calmly approached him and said, "Tommy, if you are a

Christian, you should obey Mom and not argue with her about this book. That is a sin." I could hardly believe my ears. What struck me most was the shepherding tone of his voice. He wasn't being snarky or bossy. He was gently trying to show Tommy the error of his ways. It was a remarkable moment for me as a Mom. Is there anything cooler than to see your children discipling one another in love? This was yet another indication of the healing that was taking place in this child's heart.

God deeply loves these children. He has a clear plan for their lives, to redeem the sad and tragic beginnings and to make their lives a living, breathing testimony of His love. To see Him do this in the lives of our boys is both thrilling and humbling. Only in heaven will we see how God did exceedingly abundantly more in their lives than we could have ever dreamed.

CHAPTER TWELVE

Luv Is a Verb!

෴

$\mathcal{A}$s someone who has claimed belief in Christ from a very young age, I have seen many seasons in my spiritual walk with the Lord. And, as in most things in this life, as you mature, you realize how far you are from the target. I heard a college professor, Dr. Ray Locy, say once, "The more I learn, the more I realize I don't know." This holds true in our spiritual lives as well. The more we know and experience Christ in our lives, the more we see our unworthiness and the more we value the gospel of grace that has been lavished upon us.

Ephesians 2:8

For it is by grace you have been saved, through faith and this is not from yourselves; it is the gift of God.

When I was younger, this truth was very comforting to me. My salvation was secure and nothing that I did could mess that up. However, in my immaturity, what it wasn't was motivating. The magnitude of God's gift I'd received should have propelled me into *action*. My appreciation for my spiritual adoption into God's family must not be academic knowledge alone. I believe that we were created to bring glory to the Father. And if my entire purpose in life is to bring glory to my heavenly Father, then I must do more than claim Him. I must live as He lived.

The more I study the theology of my spiritual adoption, which is at the core of the gospel, the more I am overwhelmed by our Father's heart for the fatherless. I find myself with a deep desire to feel what He feels when He sees suffering and need, especially in children. He has used the adoption of our boys to teach me even more about His love for us and how He has each day of our lives mapped out for our good and His glory! It is this same love that we are to model as we live in community with others.

This knowledge guides me as a parent, and strengthens my resolve when the task before me seems too hard. Because of the gospel of grace, I am able to see my children, in all their hardness and grief, as our Father sees them. And it reminds me that as the saying goes, "There but for the grace of God go I." You see, we are all orphans in every sense that matters eternally. The trauma of sin in our lives has required an adoption, just as the trauma of our sons' lives in China required an adoption. The understanding of this spiritual adoption has given us a platform in sharing our faith with each of our sons.

I want to challenge you, my reader, to examine the fruit of your own faith journey. The plan that God has for your life will not likely look just like mine, or Tom's, but it is there. And it's so important for you to ask Him how He would have you show love to a watching and needy world. The Scriptures show us what God requires: to do justice, to love mercy, and to walk humbly with our God (Micah 6:8). Few things in my life have humbled me more than adoption. It has been one vehicle that God has used to unearth so much of the selfishness and sinful garbage in my life.

Each new child welcomed into our family required certain sacrifices. I had expected the financial sacrifices of raising another child, and had resigned myself to those, but it was the more subtle sacrifices that I was less willing to make. I didn't realize just how much *time* would need to be devoted to each child's transition. Here I was, working in full-time ministry, where I spent a large part of each day counseling families in the adoption process and preparing them to meet the needs of their own adopted children. Coming home was not a place of respite from that heavy emotional load. Rather, it was a more intense version of my work day. The moment that I entered our home, one or more needy children would race toward the door with the "Mom, can I…", or "Mom, can you help me with?" There were days when in all honesty, I wanted to stay at work because helping other people was easier than helping my own children. What I came to realize, however, was that my home *was* my ministry, my *primary* ministry. I was going to have to dig deep in the coming years and be willing to sacrifice almost all of my "me time" in order to provide a safe and consistent place for these children to finally have their needs met. I knew that I could not rely solely on Tom's presence at home with them to fill in what they were missing from me. Slowly, the Lord showed me just how desperately my sons needed a mother who was truly present with them and who was willing to give up whatever time they required.

Brothers and sisters, let us remind one another that to truly love Christ is to love others. To serve Him is to serve others. And, as the old D.C. Talk song says, "I don't care what they say, I don't care what ya heard, the word Luv? Luv is a Verb!"

5th grade graduate

CHAPTER THIRTEEN

The Day
Everything Changed

June 2, 2015 was the day our two youngest graduated from the fifth grade. The thought of us no longer having children in elementary school was a little sad, but of course, we were excited for this next stage with Tommy and Cooper. We had already decided to bring the two youngest home for school to join their three brothers who were being taught at home by their Dad. Tommy was especially excited because he knew it would allow him to move ahead more easily and study some of his favorite subjects in ways he could not in public school. After the ceremony, we took the customary family photos on the decorated benches outside. Balloons adorned each end of the bench and nice chalkboard signs were there as props. It was the same scene we'd seen the year before when Cameron finished fifth grade. The beautiful South Carolina sun was shining and it was a postcard kind of day.

We headed over to our favorite Chick-Fil-A to treat the boys to a celebratory lunch. I got in line, knowing already what each child would want. Tom stood beside me while the boys scoped out a table. As the line got shorter, I asked Tom what he felt like eating that day and he said, "Nothing." Wait. What? Tom Rylands never eats nothing. I asked him why and he said something like, "I'm just not hungry". Again, very out of character, especially at lunchtime. His tone made it clear that this was not the time to probe, so I ordered the kids' lunches and we sat and ate. When we finished, we loaded up the van and headed home to enjoy the afternoon together.

Throughout the afternoon, Tom was a little slower than normal and looked tired. He prepared a nice dinner for us but again, despite fixing himself a plate, he didn't eat. I started to worry. When I asked him what was wrong, he told me that he was having trouble swallowing. This was the same thing he'd complained of two months earlier when we had taken the kids to Myrtle Beach for the day, that and some discomfort in his chest. Playing things safe, we'd left the Kids' Museum that day and taken Tom to the Emergency Room, but after 24 hours of observation, we were told to consult with a gastrointestinal doctor once we got home, because his heart was fine. Tom did make an appointment, but had to wait six weeks to be seen as a new patient.

So, here we were with the same chief complaint, only this time, he was getting paler and weaker than before. I no longer felt okay with him waiting for that appointment. Knowing he would resist, I told him that I wanted to take Tommy to our local Health First because he'd been coughing a lot. I said, "Hey, you don't look good. Why don't you just ride along with Tommy and me and have the doctor check you out too?" Thankfully, he agreed and we rode the four miles to the doctor's office.

When we arrived, Tom was looking dramatically worse and complaining of breathing troubles. I grabbed a doctor and had him come right in to check him out. They were all bewildered when his oxygen levels read 98%. Clearly he was getting enough oxygen. This is where the fast actions of an experienced ER doctor came into play. He took some blood and did a soft tissue chest x-ray. Within minutes, he calmly entered our room and recommended that we take Tom down to the ER for a CT scan. He told us that his white blood cell count was very high. I learned that normal counts are under 10,000 and Tom's was almost 21,000. He was so concerned that when I asked if we had time to run Tommy back home, he did not recommend it.

I didn't realize it at the time, but as we headed to the car and drove to the hospital in silence, our world slowed to a crawl. It was like wading through a dream. There was nothing productive to be said. We both anticipated something awful and didn't dare speculate on what it might be. We arrived at the ER around 7:00 pm and had the CT scan. The results came quickly…almost too quickly. The scan showed a large tumor that was located near his heart and also some areas of concern on the lung and liver. We learned that the tumor was partially wrapped around his aorta and fighting for space with his heart. There was much we didn't know at this point, but we knew it was very serious.

This began what was to be a two-week hospital stay that would include several biopsy surgeries, emergency heart surgery and a hospital transfer. What had started as a day of celebration ended in tragedy as I held onto Tom's hand and somberly took in the doctors' every word.

Little did we know, as we smiled for the camera that morning, that it was our last "normal" day as a family of seven. None of us knew then about the huge, aggressive tumor sitting on my husband's heart. We didn't know that in five short hours, I'd be rushing him to the ER where we would hear the most dreadful words, "Mr. Rylands, you have a very large tumor in your chest." In that moment, our entire world came to a screeching halt.

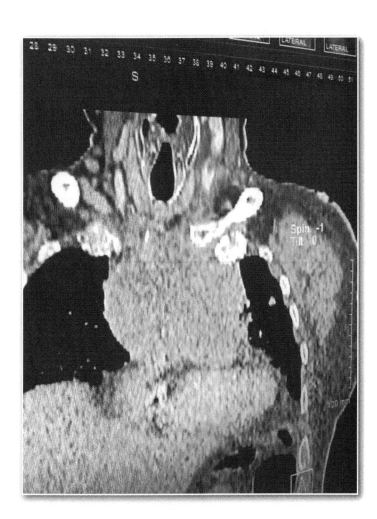

CHAPTER FOURTEEN

Cancer

᪐

Cancer. It is a word that we have become almost numb to in our everyday lives. It is so common that it almost doesn't elicit a reaction at all, until it is associated with you or someone you hold dear.

Then, it has grave meaning. Then, it is ugly and vile and sneaky and becomes the focus of your every thought. Cancer.

Upon receiving the news of this large tumor in Tom's chest, fighting for space to grow, and pressing up against his trachea, everything began moving in slow motion. In less than two days, we saw an oncologist who uttered the words that still ring in my ears: Stage Four Cancer. I'm not entirely sure I was breathing in this moment. I couldn't wrap my head around what that meant. I knew virtually nothing about cancer and that's the way I liked it! What did this mean? Was it treatable? What kind of cancer did he have? Was it operable? The questions that swirled through my mind were, no doubt, the same questions that countless patients and their families have asked doctors for decades.

Of course, our doctor answered our questions to the best of his ability, but there was so much that he didn't know yet. Most importantly, without a biopsy of the tumor, he had no way to definitively diagnose this beast. And I needed it to have a name.

We began with a decision to biopsy the liver, as it was the least risky access point. The doctors believed that this would give us the answers we needed to create a treatment plan. The procedure itself went smoothly, but the results would not be immediate.

As I was in the waiting room with more than a dozen precious friends, buried in a sea of prayers, Tom was brought back up with the expectation that he'd finally be allowed to eat something. He hadn't had a bite to eat since breakfast on Tuesday and we were now nearing dinnertime Thursday. He was hungry and didn't mind you knowing it, thank you very much.

As we waited for his tray to arrive, the echocardiogram tech came in to take a look at his heart. I thought nothing of it, as we were becoming quite accustomed to tests and pokes. Finally, his pork chop and sweet potato arrived. I helped cut it up for him since he was still very weak, and lifted the fork to his mouth. Halfway to my target, the doctor raced in and said, "Stop! I'm very sorry, Mr. Rylands, but you can't eat that. You need emergency heart surgery and we have called an ambulance to take you to another hospital with a highly qualified thoracic surgeon who can perform the procedure you need. You will leave within 30 minutes." We had no time to even think. I was instructed to pack our things and head to the other hospital and that the ambulance would meet me there. Only later in the day would I learn that Tom's heart rate was dangerously high.

Within ten minutes I was racing down the road, calling key friends and family to spread the news that we were in dire need of prayer. In addition to this tumor that was choking the life out of him, Tom had experienced massive fluid buildup around his heart inside his pericardium. Since the pericardium does not stretch, the result was pressure squeezing the heart. They had to operate to release that fluid and reduce the pressure. Tom arrived and the surgeon skillfully performed the procedure. Once it was completed, the decision was made to keep Tom sedated and on the ventilator for the next several days, in ICU, so that his body could heal more quickly. His entire team agreed that he needed rest first and foremost due to the intense trauma of the last few days.

What lonely days those were. I was so thankful each time someone would come and just sit with me. Seeing Tom lying there unconscious and breathing on a ventilator was very hard. This man, larger than life itself, my best friend, was weak and frail and so very, very sick. Having to be buzzed into this locked ward each time I left to catch my breath or use the restroom was tiring, and for health reasons, it was a very sterile environment, with little decor to cheer one up.

Late Friday we finally received the results of the liver biopsy, but they proved unhelpful. In fact, the results puzzled Tom's entire team. They indicated his diagnosis as primary liver cancer. But no one on his medical team had ever seen liver cancer present itself in the form of a massive mediastinal ("between the lungs") tumor. In order to solve this mystery, it became necessary to operate again -- immediately. They called in an entire surgical team for Saturday morning, when they do not typically operate, along with a pathologist so they could work on a diagnosis. The procedure didn't take long, but they had to go into his chest from right below his left shoulder and extract a sample from the tumor. I was grateful that he was at least still intubated and that it wasn't necessary to do that again.

After the procedure, the pathologist, upon initial evaluation, did not think that the tumor was at all related to the liver biopsy. What that meant was that it was not the same cancer! While they admitted it was rare, it appeared that Tom had two completely different cancers in his body. (No one ever accused Tom Rylands of doing things the "normal" way!) They were able to take Tom off the ventilator by Saturday afternoon and he had a nice visit with his two grown daughters.

Though we were hopeful each day that we would have a name for this cancer that had so rudely invaded our lives, we waited in vain. I would soon learn just how rare a cancer this was and that each test was in essence, peeling off one more layer of the onion. It was a process of elimination to see how the cells were behaving.

Finally, on Monday, we were transferred out of ICU and into a transition room on the post-surgical cardiac floor. Though these were harder days for Tom than those he spent unconscious, it was nice to finally have our own room and to have him awake and talking to me. Due to the demands on his heart and the challenges of recovering from surgery, our main focus had temporarily shifted. At this point, his only goal was to heal from major surgery and to get stronger. He was not the best patient in this regard as he absolutely loathed the hourly breathing exercises they wanted him to do. And still, each day passed with no official diagnosis.

By Wednesday, we were sent from the heart floor to the oncology floor. It was a tiny room, but it was private and much more comfortable. The nurses on this floor were angels, truly. We would stay another week in the hospital there before finally being discharged to come home.

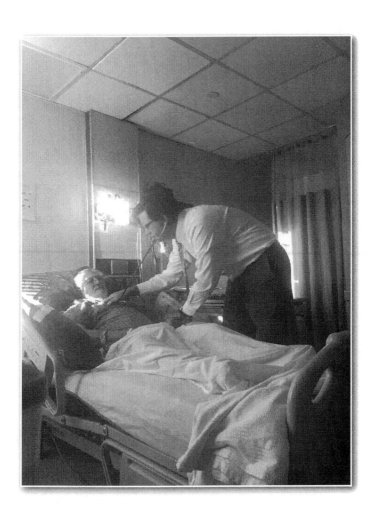

CHAPTER FIFTEEN

Diagnosis and Prognosis

☙

All this time, well over a week, our children had not been allowed to see their Dad. Once Tom was out for the night, I would slip home and get what little sleep I could and be back before dawn so I didn't miss the physicians on their rounds. My mom and other friends helped with the boys almost around the clock for over a week. We had shared bits and pieces with the boys, but at this point, they were not aware of just how serious their Dad's situation really was.

Finally, Tom was strong enough for the boys to come see him. They were all worried and had missed him terribly. I could see how nervous they were to be there and to see their Dad not looking like "Dad." But Tom put on a brave face and big smile for their visit and it went well. It did my heart good to see them together.

By this time, still without a firm diagnosis, our oncologist told me that Tom was not going to get better. He was sound asleep when the doctor came by, so I asked some more probing questions. The treatment plan then was radiation therapy, and later, once those treatments were complete, chemotherapy. The doctor needed me to know that this was a measure that they hoped would prolong his time with us, but that he did not have an expectation that it would be curable. What the pathology had shown them so far was that this was a new and very aggressive tumor. In no more than three to six months, it had grown to the size of a grapefruit in his chest. That is fast! Their main goal was to retard that growth and give him more time. Of course, there was no way for him to tell me how long he had, but what he did say with more confidence was that we probably didn't have even another year. Having to share this news with Tom's daughter, Krisha, was one of the hardest phone calls I've ever made.

Finally on June 16, 2015, we had a ***name***! That's right, we finally had a completed pathology report complete with a diagnosis.

Primitive (or poorly differentiated) Neuroendocrine Tumor (of the Lung)

He did say that these kinds of tumors are very, very rare which is why it took a week and a half to get a diagnosis.

After two weeks in the hospital, Tom was able to come home. We went out for radiation treatments a few times a week. Just getting him from the door to the car was exhausting. By the end of the second week home, it became clear that he was getting too weak to continue. In fact, he was so weak by his last scheduled treatment that it had to be cancelled.

The day of that final treatment, Tom and I left the hospital and went straight to see Dr. Rose, his oncologist. It was that meeting, the one where we ask the hard questions and get even harder answers. It was the day we heard – and finally accepted -- that my precious husband was dying.

How can something seem so very real and yet impossible at the same time? Medically speaking, it was a question of when, not if. We were given no hope, outside of a decision from God to intervene, that Tom would survive.

It was also at this meeting that the doctor recommended that they send out a palliative care team to the house to address issues of comfort as we moved ahead. They were the professionals who would meet with us about ways to make Tom's quality of life as enjoyable as possible for the time that remained.

Of course, while all these things were important realities, the biggest thing weighing on our hearts was, of
course, our family. Tom called his daughters and gave
them the news. What emotional conversations! The bigger challenge would be telling our sons. They had been
through so much already in their young lives and so this
news, while always devastating, would be increasingly so
due to the compounding effect of this additional trauma.

We knew that we could not wait too long to tell them
what we knew. They deserved time to fully comprehend
this, and to soak up every day with their Dad that they
could. But, we also knew that they would need a strong
support system beyond us. One of my greatest fears was
the knowledge that I could not fix this for any of them
and that I would not be able to meet all of their emotional needs as we walked this out. I was relying on God to
supernaturally strengthen and support our children. We
were counting on the body of Christ to love our children
well as we all grieved.

As we left for home, Tom asked me to drive the long
way, over the intracoastal waterway. He looked me in the
eye and said, "I'm never going to leave the house again
and I want to see the water one last time." My heart was
so heavy. I drove over that bridge as we both looked out
over the gleaming water. It was a classic Charleston
summer day and it was stunning. Down below us were
boats cutting through the water and shimmers of light

reflecting up at us. I wanted so badly to take Tom to see the ocean one last time, to stand together with our toes in the sand. It was unquestionably his favorite place in the world. When I offered to take him, he refused. I knew it would be hard to navigate his wheelchair over the dunes, but I was confident that we could get an army of men, if need be, to get him there. Sadly, he reminded me of the intense humidity and the strain it was for him to breathe now. So, much to my disappointment, we decided that it was just too late for that. My heart ached that I could not grant him that one final blessing.

CHAPTER SIXTEEN

Telling the Boys

❧

*T*wo days later, Tom announced that he was ready to tell the boys about his prognosis, to tell them that he was dying. I know this would be a weighty decision for anyone in our situation, but an extra layer for us was the extensive work we'd had just building trust with our sons. That was hard, given their backgrounds and the many times that adults had disappointed them. So, we could not risk even the perception of dishonesty as it would have put all our hard work at risk. We had to tell them what we knew.

Tom decided that he wanted his eldest daughter to be here as well as her husband, both of whom had arrived from Virginia the night before, and he also wanted the boys' karate Sensei to be there to support them. So, we called Sensei over and we gathered the kids around the living room for the most difficult family meeting of our lives.

Tom was sitting up in a wheelchair, with Sensei seated at his right facing the boys, and Krisha on the sofa. At first, I was seated on the hospital bed to his left. Neither of us has ever done anything as hard as telling our sons that their father was dying and that we did not know when it would happen. Tom was quick to tell the boys that doctors are not God and that we do not know if He intends to work a miracle and spare his life or if He is ready to call him home, but that no matter the outcome, no matter the time frame, the name of the Lord is to be praised. What a powerful reminder in an incredibly challenging time. Never in my life have I been so proud of my husband as I was that night.

I don't think any of the adults in the room really had any idea how this would go. We did have the foresight to load the room with tissues, which turned out to be a wise decision. There are few things harder in this life as a parent than to watch your children in pain. Not surprisingly, Tommy and Cooper (our two youngest, ten and twelve at the time) broke down first. Tom's daughter scooped up Cooper and loved him well as he listened to this awful news. I held Tommy as he cried. Our older boys listened intently and processed this news each in his own way. Tom spoke with such composure and peace as he shared his love for the Lord and his thoughts about his own mortality. He challenged them to love one another well, now and after he went to be with the Lord. He reminded them of a time, shortly after each had come into our family, when he told them of God's good and perfect plan and how being adopted into our family was a part of that plan. Heads nodded around the room as each boy remembered those conversations. Tom proceeded to tell them that this, this incredibly sad and hard news, was also part of His perfect plan. He looked our children in the eye and told them that God was calling him home and that his death would be part of God's plan for their lives and they could rest in that knowledge when it was hard. It was the holiest moment of my life. Seeing Sensei, a dear friend of our family, sitting next to Tom, emotionally holding him up as he spoke, assuring the boys that they would always have a spiritual family that would care for them no matter what, was an unexpected blessing.

It was an honor to experience this moment with our beloved family. Tom's daughter was amazing as she encouraged the boys not to hide from their feelings, whatever they may be from moment to moment. She told them that it was okay to feel whatever comes and that the Lord would draw near to them. The way she loved our sons that night was a tribute to her love for her father, and really honored him. I was so grateful we decided not to wait until they left for home. This was exactly as it was meant to be.

When Tom was finished talking to the children, he asked if anyone had any questions. At first the room was quiet. Only the labored breathing of our crying could be heard. Then our fifteen–year-old son Connor said, "Dad, where will you be?" I suppose he could tell by our expression that we were confused, so he said, "I mean, which house will be yours?" Almost in unison, we realized that our son, home barely two years then, was asking about his heavenly mansion. He said, "The Bible says that God has a house prepared for you. Where will it be?" Tom smiled and replied, "I don't know, baby, but I'm sure it will be in the Rylands' Suite, so I won't be hard to find." Oh how it blessed my heart to hear my "hardest" child, my most protective and shut-off child, processing his father's impending death through a heavenly lens!

While none of us knew exactly the hour that the Lord would call Tom home, he knew that it would be soon. So, it became increasingly urgent to him that he tend to things that would make his passing easier on us all. As any good husband would, Tom wanted to make sure that I was prepared and well cared for when he died. Now, I'm not talking financially so much, but rather, emotionally, spiritually and in the practical daily life of raising five boys alone. These were the things that occupied his mind in those last few weeks.

Each day, it seemed, he would call someone with whom he wanted to meet. One such meeting was with our sons' pastors. He called these two young men to our home, one responsible for the middle school ministry and the other working with the high school students. I remember the three of us taking chairs and lining up beside Tom's hospital bed in the living room as he began to explain the gravity of what was about to transpire.

Tom shared very bluntly with these men that he was going to die soon. He told them that he expected them to lovingly and intentionally disciple his sons. He went on to share with them some of the boys' background and things that he imagined they would struggle with once he died. He talked about their personalities and how they handle struggles and heartache. He shared some of their favorite things to do and charged these two men with the privilege and responsibility of looking after his sons when he was no longer able. It was a somber conversation, but one that they handled with great maturity. They actually thanked Tom for meeting with them and for loving our sons enough to ensure that their spiritual walks weren't ignored. Tom could rest more easily knowing that there would be men taking hold of our boys and being intentional about time with them.

Tom also met with some of his musician buddies from church. You see, Tom was very purposeful about the kind of memorial service he wanted. He was characterized throughout his life as a funny, funny man. He loved to make people laugh. He would not abide a sad and depressing service. So, one by one, he shared the songs and even the jokes that he wanted told at his service.

It was quite surreal for me to walk past the living room and hear him planning his own funeral, but that was Tom. He did not want any unnecessary burdens placed on me, so he took care of many things before he died, while he still could. He even dictated his own obituary so I would not have to do it alone.

Our living room had become my new home. Since bringing Tom home from the hospital, we rarely left this room. It was our parlor in which we visited with guests. It was our dining room where I urged Tom to eat whenever he had an appetite. It was our new bedroom. For over a month, this was where we stayed, Tom in his hospital bed and I on the sectional sofa. As I looked up one day to the large family portrait that hung over our fireplace, I began to see a future without Tom in the photographs. This was a hard reality to comprehend. I spoke with a neighbor and brother in Christ who is a photographer and he offered to take a family photo if Tom was able. I so wanted the boys to have one more chance to get a nice picture with their dad, so we arranged to take him to our neighborhood clubhouse and get one last large family picture taken. Thankfully, Krisha and her family were able to participate as well, so they also made some precious memories that day. That forty-five minutes was incredibly draining for Tom, and it took every ounce of strength he had to make it through, but he did it, for us. But, then, why would I expect anything less of this man in his death than he gave in his vibrant years? He was serving us literally until his body no longer allowed it.

Perhaps the most important thing that Tom did while he still could was the taping of audio messages for two of his grandsons and our five boys. We got a recording app on his phone and one at a time, over the course of a week or more, when a spurt of energy would come, he'd get out that phone and start talking to one of the boys. I can't express what a treasure that was for this Mama. When they were ready, our boys were able to listen to their father's final words to them. He encouraged them in their faith. He instructed them to love and care for their mother and to disciple and encourage one another. He recalled favorite memories he'd shared with each of them. It is a gift that many do not get when they lose a parent, and I'm forever grateful our boys will have these to listen to whenever they need their Dad close.

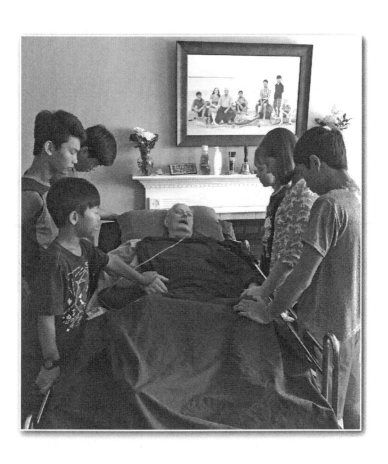

CHAPTER SEVENTEEN

Goodbye, My Love

❧

*I*t was shocking how rapidly Tom's health declined after the night we talked to the boys. Much of what transpired over the course of the next two weeks is a blur. I'm thankful that we understood the gravity, however, as it informed many of our decisions in those days and allowed us to shift priorities as needed.

Tom's eldest daughter was a rock for me during this time. She and her family drove down from Virginia every weekend for four straight weeks and as the last days approached, she extended her stay as long as she could.

It was because of her that I was able to get the occasional night's sleep in my own bed and actually rest. She stayed with Tom when I had to go out, and most of all, she was a treasured light for him when he needed her love the most.

There were so many people who loved Tom and me. Many folks served us and prayed for us during these last days, but only Krisha could understand the deep pain of watching her father fade away before our eyes. You see, he was her hero every bit as much as he was mine. While our relationship with him was so different, the depth of our love for him was much the same. It was a strong, yet strange bond that grew in those weeks. I never anticipated that we'd be tending to Tom together as he died, but I know it gave him great joy.

After putting her departure off day after day, not knowing what the next hours would hold, it was finally time for them to head home. They had a business to run and employees to pay. Krisha reminded me of how difficult it was to handle him alone now that he was so weak, so we called the hospice nurse and asked someone to come assess him.

It was decided that it was time for someone to stay with me around the clock, so our amazing nurse, Lori, came the next morning to stay. Then Krisha felt she could safely leave. That was Tuesday.

The following morning, July 8, 2015, our sweet neighbor called to invite the boys out to the beach for a much-needed distraction. All but Connor decided to go. Before they left, I called the boys in and we surrounded Tom's bed. I encouraged the boys to pray for their father and let them know that it was not going to be long before he went to heaven. I can't adequately describe the sacredness of that time. One by one, our boys offered prayers of thanksgiving for their father and asked for peace and rest. We all laid hands on this incredible patriarch hoping that he was listening to the love of his family as he slept. Everyone except Tommy took turns to pray for Tom. Our precious little one just couldn't bring himself to speak the words. I held Tommy tightly as I held Tom's hand and prayed.

The children left and the house was quiet except for Tom's intermittent gasping for breath and his groaning from heavy medication. Those sounds, so unsettling at first, had now grown familiar. The most difficult decision I had to make that day was whether or not to continue the heavy doses of morphine. You see, I desperately wanted to speak to Tom. I ached to hear his voice one last time. But, I knew that if I let up on the medicine, he'd become disoriented and fearful. Seeing him suffer was more than I could bear, so I kept him sedated till the end.

It was clear that it wouldn't be long. His oxygen levels had continued to fall and his breaths were more and more spread out. Tom's best friend Bob came over to the house to go over his eulogy with me. He read it out loud, to practice his delivery as well as for Tom's sake. It was perfect. It was everything Tom had wanted, and in that moment, my precious husband took his last breath.

The hospice nurse commented that he was waiting to hear the end of the eulogy. Knowing Tom, she was likely right. Either way, it made me smile. I leaned over him and said, "Goodbye, my love."

As if on cue, I received a text from my neighbor that the boys were on their way back home from the beach. There was no time to stay in the moment and be alone with all of this. The children were coming and I had to prepare them. There were phone calls to make to family. There were now all the things that we knew would come and there was very little time to stop and process any of it. I decided that it was best for them not to see their father like that, so I met them outside in the yard, along with our worship pastor, and escorted them into the front office of our home. It was then that I had the painful task of telling our five boys that their father was in heaven. Each took the news in their own way. Cameron began to weep deeply. Cooper smiled broadly and announced to all of us that "Dad is with Jesus now and he will never hurt again!" Tommy and Connor withdrew into silent reverence and Colin, true to his character, began to care for everyone else. Even then, God was already meeting their needs. The youth pastors were notified and they came to be with the boys and show their support.

The funeral home sent staff to take his body away. The first question they asked was whether Tom was a U.S. Veteran. As it happened, both men who came for him were themselves vets. They draped him in the most crisp American flag I'd ever seen, and rolled him out of our home. It was one of the most solemn moments of my life. There was great grief, intermingled with profound pride and gratitude for having been this man's wife, fears about what lay ahead for us as a family and a strange peace that could only come from God. Never have I experienced so many seemingly contradictory emotions at one time. I didn't know then how common this would be in the months ahead.

His memorial service was unforgettable. To see over three hundred people pour in to shower us with love and respect was very moving. The music was fit for a Presidential funeral. A full orchestra, saxophone ensemble, and Tom's "Little Big Band" all performed and it was such a blessing to me. All volunteered their time to pay tribute to this incredible musician who had influenced them for years. I remember as I arrived at the church, walking into the sanctuary alone and hearing the orchestra warming up. At the front of the room was a large floral arrangement, a perfectly placed American flag and a picture of our family on a large easel. I stood silent for several minutes scanning the stage, watching each person practice with intensity, and I remember wondering if Tom was looking down and smiling as I was.

CHAPTER EIGHTEEN

Trusting Abba Father

꧁

*H*undreds of cards and letters, gifts and financial donations filled our mailbox as God used His people to meet our emotional and practical needs. And He is so intentional, our God. Each gift seemed targeted to a specific need of which the giver was unaware. Car repairs, health insurance, gas cards and more were taken care of by people all over the United States. And the lesson that this taught our sons was one that neither Tom nor I could ever have taught them ourselves. What they learned, and are still learning to this day, is that the body of Christ is meant to love and care for one another, and it is remarkable when they do just that! This was a lesson to be learned firsthand. It isn't something that you can just talk about. An often overlooked portion of the verse in Ephesians 3: 21 is "to Him be glory in the church." What our family has experienced through our local body of believers has caused me to adore my Abba Father so much more. These Christ-followers, through their service to us, have allowed God's glory to shine through them in remarkable ways. My prayer for everyone who reads this book and claims the name of Christ is that they would be people who serve one another sacrificially. You may never know the impact you could have on the generation that follows or the watching world desperately seeking meaning and truth in their lives. You never know when God might desire to use you to bless someone else abundantly more than they could ask or imagine.

Many times I've been told how strong I am. But I am just like you. We are all weak and frail in the face of this kind of loss. We are all broken and in need of daily -- no, hourly -- support from a loving God. There are times in the midst of deep grief and pain that you just can't see past the moment you are in. I know now that it's okay to be there.

I made very few commitments those first few months after losing Tom. I knew it was important to give myself the freedom to do, or not do, whatever was best for the boys and me *that day*. This was not an easy thing to accept at first. That person I described in the early chapters of this book, that go-getter, that fixer, that doer… she still wanted to come out. She still wanted to exist, but part of her was so wounded that she needed to hibernate and heal for a season.

Never in my life had I faced the kinds of decisions as I faced after the death of my husband. Not parenting, not school, not career choices. None of these major life moments created in me the same vacuum as having to say goodbye to Tom. He was the glue that kept our family together and functioning well.

Over the years, I'd often get asked, "How do you *do* it?", referring to my full-time ministry position, raising five children, etc. My answer was always, "Tom! He is amazing and serves our family so well." It's true. I could not have adopted, much less raised, these boys in our early years without this amazing man by my side. I could not have served in ministry (read: full, full-time work!) without his sacrifices and blessing. So what now? What does all this look like now that he is gone?

God has taught me so much since Tom's death. He has reinforced many things that I knew as truth, but which now reignite my love for Him. He has shown me that the truth of His Word remains ever constant and that my feelings, while important and valid, are ever-changing and unreliable.

The Bible talks quite a bit about caring for widows and orphans. By God's grace, I've had many opportunities, both personally and professionally, to care for orphans. And from time to time, though brief and fleeting, I've even had a hand in caring for a widow.

And since Tom's illness and death, I have experienced

what it is like to be truly cared for by the body of Christ. What I've realized though, is that I have no idea how to *be* the widow. Nowhere did I learn how to be the one in need, great and constant need. I was trained how to care for others, how to love and not hurt widows and orphans. But despite Tom's age and mine, I was never truly prepared to *be* his widow.

Each time someone asks me what I need, or how they can help, though the answer is always there, the words get stuck in my throat and I have to force them out. I am constantly at war between what I feel and what I know.

There are days when I feel sick, empty, wounded, weak in spirit, and deeply, deeply sad. I feel completely inadequate for the task of raising our five boys alone. I feel angry. Not that the Lord took Tom. Honestly, I am at peace with that. But, I'm angry that I feel weak. I don't like being weak. I don't like knowing that no matter how amazing I am as a mother, I will never be able to give them what a father can. I feel like I can never do enough or be enough to meet the needs of my children to whom I want to give everything. No one knows the value of a father in the lives of his sons more than I do! I saw Tom Rylands love and care for our boys when they were completely unlovable and it was like watching Christ love me. That is what I *feel*.

What I *know* is that God is using this to mold me. He is allowing me to be here, in these exact circumstances, for my good. I know this to be truth because His Word makes this promise to me. I also know that those who are giving of their time and talents to our family right now will be blessed. I know this because I have been there. I know because God has blessed me immeasurably when I've had the chance to bless others. I have always received more back from God than anything I gave. I also know that it is an act of obedience to joyfully and graciously accept these gifts, for to begrudge them, even a little, is to say that God's providence in my life is not sufficient. It would be to rob others of God's blessing in their lives. I also know that I am not enough. I never will be. God desires me to lean on Him and if I were enough, by myself, I would be less inclined to see that I need a Savior.

So as I read God's commands to embrace widows and orphans, I am reminded that this is much bigger than meeting a practical need. He uses these commands and these circumstances for a much bigger purpose.

I've reflected a great deal on my life since Tom became ill. I've come to realize that each time in my life that I had to decide whether or not to trust Abba Father, for each mundane, daily decision that had to be made, God was reinforcing in me the ability to trust Him *now*.

Friends, it is the boring tasks and the daily duties that build up our spiritual muscles. For when the big things come, we need to be able to blindly fall backwards into those arms that have steadied us so many times before. It is precisely because God has guided our family through countless bumps in the road that I can honestly say that I trust Him to be Abba to us now. I trust Him to be provider as I obey His call to leave my full-time position and homeschool our children in Tom's place. I trust Him to once again be the Father to the fatherless in our home. I trust Him to hold me when I ache for strong arms around me. I trust Him to bring healing and hope and joy into our lives, and I trust Him to fill every crack and gap in me so that I can serve my family well.

This story is not the one that I thought I'd be telling at 44. I truly didn't see this coming. But this isn't where our story ends. How do I know this? First, because my 72–year-old husband would laugh at me for thinking such a thing at my age. Second, because God has confirmed in my heart that He isn't done yet. Tom's death does not mean the end for us, though our hearts are so torn. There's so much more that's yet to unfold. As we wait on Him and see where He will lead us next, we will cling to His promises with joy. I will choose to endure in this season and trust God. For He is faithful and His plans are always better than ours. He is the God who is able to do far more abundantly than all that we ask or think, and He isn't finished with us yet. Oh, the joy of expecting *Abundantly More*.

Photos

My Dad's original cornet played by me in
middle school. Now, Tommy plays it.

Liberty University Brass Quintet @1990

Christmas CD recorded in 2004 with *Treasures of Grace*.
I was 5 months pregnant when it was released.

Treasures of Grace in recording studio, Spring 2004

Our Wedding Day, January 25, 2001

Our last posed picture together, June 27, 2015

Tom and Angie at the beach, pregnant with Tommy
Summer 2004

Tom and Tommy, home from the hospital
November 2004

Our little "turkey", 7 months old

Tommy, 10 months old

"Twas the Night Before Christmas"

Chef Tommy helping Mommy bake brownies

Tommy, 2 years old

Tom and Angie, 2001

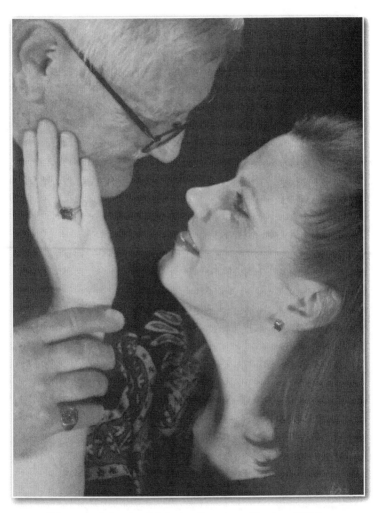

Tom and Angie, 10th Anniversary Cruise, 2011

First family of four photo, August 22, 2011

Tom buying water at Wal-Mart in Shenyang, China, 2011

Tommy with big brother, Colin, touring his "finding place."

Colin and Tommy in traditional Mongolian
dress. Represents Colin's ancestry

Tommy's first chopsticks experience

Family tour day, August 2011

The boys touring some historical gardens, August 2011

Colin, Angie, Cameron on Cameron's adoption day,
December 12, 2011, Wuhan, China

Angie, Connor, Cameron on Connor's adoption day,
March 11, 2013 in Chongqing, China.

Angie and Cooper signing adoption papers,
March 13, 2013, in Changsha, China

Rylands' boys on Isle of Palms beach, Summer 2013

Connor, Colin, Cameron, Cooper, Tommy at
Point Judith Lighthouse, Rhode Island, October 2015
Paying respects to their father at one of his favorite places.

Cameron, Cooper, Colin, Tommy, Connor
Christmas morning, 2014

Cameron, Tommy, Colin, Cooper, Connor
Fort Moultrie, Sullivan's Island, SC, May 2014

Connor, Cooper, Tommy, Cameron, Colin
Christmas 2015

About the Author

*A*ngie Rylands received a BA in music education from Liberty University in Lynchburg, Virginia, her hometown. Between 2011 and 2013, she and her husband Tom adopted four sons from China, which was an experience that helped inspire her eventual employment with the team at Lifeline Children's Services. She served there as South Carolina State Director until her husband's death in 2015. Angie now homeschools their children full-time, and also serves as a consultant and public speaker for foster care and adoption ministries around the country.

Made in the USA
Charleston, SC
26 July 2016